AF600150

THE LOCAL SUPERIOR IN NON-EXEMPT CLERICAL CONGREGATIONS

THE CATHOLIC UNIVERSITY OF AMERICA
CANON LAW STUDIES
No. 351

The Local Superior in Non-Exempt Clerical Congregations

A HISTORICAL CONSPECTUS AND A COMMENTARY

A DISSERTATION
SUBMITTED TO THE FACULTY OF THE SCHOOL OF CANON LAW OF THE CATHOLIC UNIVERSITY OF AMERICA IN PARTIAL FULFILLMENT OF THE REQUIREMENTS FOR THE DEGREE OF DOCTOR OF CANON LAW

BY
ROBERT EAMON McGRATH, O.M.I., J.C.L.
PRIEST OF ST. PETER'S PROVINCE

THE CATHOLIC UNIVERSITY OF AMERICA PRESS
WASHINGTON, D.C.
1954

Nihil Obstat:
A. MacInnes, O.M.I., S.T.L.,
R. Luckhart, O.M.I., S.T.L.,
Censores Deputati.

Imprimi Potest:
Fergus O'Grady, O.M.I.,
Superior Provincialis.

Ottavae, Ont., die 20 aprilis, 1955.

Nihil Obstat:
Romaeus W. O'Brien, O. Carm., J.C.D.,
Censor Deputatus.

Imprimatur:
✠ Patricius A. O'Boyle, D.D.,
Archiepiscopus Washingtonensis.

Washingtonii. D.C., die 18 aprilis, 1955.

Printed by
Le Droit Printers and Publishers
Ottawa, Ontario,
Canada.

89

TABLE OF CONTENTS

FOREWORD

In undertaking to write this dissertation the writer proposes to collect in one work and to comment on the principal laws of the Code of Canon Law which deal with the local superior in a non-exempt clerical Congregation of pontifical approval. The local superior in an exempt Order of men has been made the subject of a dissertation in the School of Canon Law of The Catholic University of America,[1] but many questions pertaining to the local religious superior in a non-exempt clerical Congregation have not as yet been made the subject of a special study.

In seeking to provide a historical background for this work the writer found it impractical to deal with the particular legislation concerning the local superior of each of the Congregations which had received the approval of the Holy See before the promulgation of the Code. In the absence of any general pre-Code legislation on the non-exempt religious superior, and indeed in the absence of such legislation for the government of non-exempt Congregations themselves, it was decided that Chapter I of this dissertation should be devoted to a historical conspectus of the development and laws of non-exempt Congregations.

Chapter II concerns itself with the office of the local superior and his position as the head of a particular society. Chapter III discusses the authority of the local superior, the divergent canonical theories on the foundation, nature, and extent of the superior's power, and concludes with the presentation of what is, in the writer's opinion, the most plausible theory.

The qualities required in the candidate for the office of local superior, the method of his appointment, and his term of

[1] Patrick Clancy, *The Local Religious Superior*, The Catholic University of America Canon Law Studies, n. 171 (Washington, D.C.: The Catholic Universitv of America Press, 1943).

office are treated in Chapter IV. The last Chapter presents the principal rights and obligations which are attached by common law to the office of local superior.

It is hoped that this work will be useful to those who desire to know the prescriptions of the common law regarding the local superior in a non-exempt clerical Congregation of pontifical approval. It need hardly be noted, however, that in specific instances it will be necessary to consult the approved Constitutions of each Congregation in order to see how the common law of the Church has been applied and adapted.

The writer wishes to take this opportunity to express his gratitude to his former Provincial Superior, the Very Reverend Joseph R. Birch, O.M.I., Assistant General of the Congregation of the Missionary Oblates of Mary Immaculate, for providing the opportunity to begin graduate studies in Canon Law, and to his present Provincial Superior, the Very Reverend Fergus O'Grady, O.M.I., for making it possible to continue these studies. To his fellow Oblates of the Eastern Province at the Oblate Scholasticate, Washington, D.C., he extends his appreciation for their warm Oblate hospitality over the past three years. The writer is especially grateful to Rev. Fr. Garrett Barry, O.M.I., J.C.D., professor of Canon Law and Moral Theology at the Oblate Scholasticate, Washington, D.C., for his kindness and patience and for the invaluable assistance that he has offered in the preparation of this dissertation. The writer is also grateful to the members of the Faculty of the School of Canon Law of the Catholic University of America for their clear exposition of the law of the Church. To all those who have aided the writer in his Canon Law studies, he is deeply grateful.

PART I

HISTORICAL CONSPECTUS

CHAPTER I

THE GROWTH AND JURIDICAL GOVERNMENT OF NON-EXEMPT CLERICAL CONGREGATIONS

Article 1. The Historical Development of Non-exempt Clerical Congregations

As a preliminary to the canonical commentary on the rights and duties of the local superior in papally approved non-exempt Congregations of clerics, it is considered advisable to give a brief historical conspectus of the development of the non-exempt clerical Congregation, the definition of which is given in canon 488, 2°: "In canonibus qui sequuntur, veniunt nomine: ... *Congregationis religiosæ* vel *Congregationis* simpliciter, religio in quo vota dumtaxat simplicia sive perpetua sive temporaria emittuntur."

By the thirteenth century, the religious Institutes had become so numerous that they caused confusion in the Church. The lay people, called on to aid by their alms such a multiplicity of Institutes, found the burden very great. The misguided zeal of some of the founders of these new religious organizations led their followers into heresy. In an effort to remedy these conditions Pope Innocent III (1198-1216) in the IV General Council of the Lateran (1215) declared that no new religious Institute could be founded without the approval of the Holy See. Furthermore, if one wished to become a religious, he was to join one of the existing and approved Orders, and should anyone wish to found a new monastery, he was obliged to adopt a rule of life already approved.[2]

These prescriptions of Pope Innocent were poorly observed, and a subsequent Pontiff, Gregory X (1271-1276), felt con-

---

[2] Can. 13 — Mansi, *Sacrorum Conciliorum Nova et Amplissima Collectio* (53 vols. in 60, Parisiis, 1901-1927), XXII, 1002 (hereinafter cited as Mansi); c. 9, X, *de religiosis domibus,* III, 36; Henry J. Schroeder, *Disciplinary Decrees of the General Councils* (St. Louis: B. Herder Book Co., 1937), p. 255.

strained to re-enact the laws of the General Council of the Lateran referred to above. In the 23rd canon of the II General Council of Lyons (1274) Pope Gregory once more declared that the Holy See alone could give approval to new Institutes. He then proceeded to state that all Orders, including the Mendicants, which had been founded without papal approval since the prohibition of the IV General Council of the Lateran were suppressed. Those which had received the approval of the Holy See and which were dependent for their members' livelihood on the alms of the public were not allowed to receive any more members to profession, nor could they acquire or dispose of houses without the special permission of the Apostolic See. Any violation of these prescriptions invalidated the acts so performed and the guilty ones were to incur excommunication. Members of these Orders were absolutely forbidden to preach to outsiders, to hear their confessions, or to bury them. However, the Pope made an exception to these rules and stated that the foregoing regulations did not extend to the Order of Preachers and that of the Friars Minor. The Order of Carmel and the Hermits of St. Augustine were permitted to continue until further provisions were made for them and for non-mendicants.[3] Pope John XXII (1316-1334) repeated these prohibitions.[4]

The authors are not in agreement on whether these prohibitory laws applied to the erection of Institutes in which only simple vows were taken. The majority maintained that the pro-

[3] Mansi, XXIV, 96-97; c. un., X, *de religiosis domibus,* III, 17, in VI°; Schroeder, *Disciplinary Decrees of the General Councils,* p. 351. It is of interest to note that, when Pope Boniface VIII (1294-1303) included this 23rd canon of the II General Council of Lyons in the *Liber Sextus,* he omitted the words which referred to the further provisions which Pope Gregory had intended to make in regard to the Order of Carmel and the Hermits of St. Augustine. Joannes Andreae, in his gloss on this chapter of the *Liber Sextus,* stated that it had been said that Pope Gregory did not wish to have any Mendicants except the Dominicans and the Franciscans. Cf. *Glossa* ad c. un., X, *de religiosis domibus,* III, 17, in VI°, s.v. *in solido.*

[4] Cf. c. un., *de religiosis domibus,* tit. VII, in *Extravag. Ioan. XXII.*

hibitions extended to all such simple vow Institutes.[5] Others considered that Pope Innocent III did not intend to prohibit the formation of such Institutes, since they were unknown in 1215.[6]

Even though, according to the majority of the authors, the laws of the IV General Council of the Lateran and the II General Council of Lyons did prohibit the formation, without prior papal approval, of Institutes whose members took merely simple vows, there are many instances, especially in the case of women's Congregations, in which the bishops brought these Institutes into being without permission from the Holy See. Perhaps one of the better explanations of the contradictions between the law and the practice is given by Bouix (1808-1870). He maintained that the bishops regained the power to found new Institutes (which power they had enjoyed from the Council of Chalcedon until the IV General Council of the Lateran) by reason of the contrary custom which their repeated acts invoked. This custom, with the tacit approval of the Holy See, superseded the laws of the IV General Council of the Lateran and the II General Council of Lyons on this point.[7]

---

[5] Ernricus Pirhing, *Ius Canonicum* (5 vols. in 4, Dilingae, 1676), Lib. III, tit. XXXVI, *De religiosis domibus ut Episcopo sunt subjectae,* 596-597, n. XXXIII; Craisson, *Manuale Totius Juris Canonici* (5. ed., 3 vols., Pictavii, 1877), II, 430; Dominicus Bouix, *Tractatus de Iure Regularium* (3. ed., 2 vols., Parisiis, 1882-1883), I, 201 (hereinafter cited as Bouix); Sebastianelli, *Praelectiones Iuris Canonici* (3 vols.), Vol. II, *De Personis* (2. ed., Romae, 1905), 359; *Collectanea in Usum Secretariae Sacrae Congregationis Episcoporum et Regularium* (cura A. Bizzarri Archiepiscopi Philippensis Secretarii edita, 2. ed., Romae: Ex Typographia Polyglotta, S. C. de Propaganda Fide, 1885), pp. 213, 423, 742, 798, footnote (hereinafter cited as *Collectanea*); Orth, *The Approbation of Religious Institutes,* The Catholic University of America Canon Law Studies, n. 71 (Washington, D.C.: The Catholic University of America, 1931), p. 36.

[6] A. Toso, *Ad Codicem Iuris Canonici Commentaria Minora* (5 vols., Romae: Marietti, 1920-1927), V, 14; Ioannes Chelodi, *Ius Canonicum de Personis* (3. ed., curavit Pius Ciprotti, Vicenza: Società anonima tipografica; Trento: A. Ardesi, 1942), p. 389, nota n. 2.

[7] Bouix, I, 210, 326.

Despite the fact that the bishops set up these new Institutes in which the common life was led, and in which the members wore a distinct garb and professed the three simple vows of poverty, chastity and obedience, there was a reluctance to regard the members of such Institutes as "religious." The reason for this reluctance was the fact that the members of these new Institutes did not take solemn vows. In the opinion of many canonical authorities as cited by Suarez (1548-1617), solemn vows were of the very essence of the religious life.[8] In fact, since Pope Boniface VIII had declared that the vows taken in religious Institutes approved by the Holy See were solemn,[9] and since Pope Innocent III had declared that those who wished to become religious were to enter one of the Institutes approved by the Holy See,[10] it seemed certain that only those who were professed with solemn vows could be considered religious in the strict juridical sense.

These commonly accepted views were greatly shaken by the action of Pope Gregory XIII (1572-1585) in reference to the simple vows of the Jesuits. The Jesuits had been approved by Pope Paul III (1534-1549) in 1540.[11] In 1550 Pope Julius III (1550-1555) allowed the practice whereby certain members of the Society of Jesus took merely simple vows.[12] Because of the prevailing opinion that only with solemn vows could one be constituted in the religious state, there were many who maintained that such Jesuits with simple vows were not religious. In 1583 Pope Gregory XIII recognized the simple vows of the Jesuits as being truly religious vows, and declared that those who had taken these simple vows were in fact religious in the

---

8 Suarez, *Opera Omnia* (28 vols., Parisiis, 1856-1878), *De statu perfectionis et religionis,* Tr. VII, lib. II, c. 14, n. 2 — Vol. XV, 181.

9 Cf. c. un., *de voto et voti redemptione,* III, 15, in VI°.

10 Cf. *supra,* p. 3.

11 Cf. *Bullarum Diplomatum et Privilegiorum Romanorum Pontificum Taurinensis Editio* (24 vols., et Appendix, Augustae Taurinorum, 1857-1872), VI, 303-306 (hereinafter cited as *Bull. Rom. Taur.).*

12 *Bull. Rom. Taur.,* VI, 425-426.

strict sense.[13] Despite the statement from the Holy See, the reluctance to consider Jesuits with simple vows as religious persisted. Pope Gregory XIII issued another Constitution and threatened with excommunication those who sought to continue the dispute or who refused to accept the statements he had made in his Constitution *Quam fructuosius.*

The Council of Trent (1545-1563) did not deal with the question of Congregations of simple vows. The twenty-fifth session of the Council concerned itself almost exclusively with the reform of the religious Orders in which solemn vows were taken. In a later portion of the present work it will be seen that portions of the legislation enacted by the Council of Trent for solemn vow Institutes were applied, during the nineteenth century, to simple vow Institutes.[14]

During the sixteenth century, contrary to the legislation of the IV General Council of the Lateran and the II General Council of Lyons, as cited above, there arose communities whose members took only simple vows.[15] Consequently, Pope St. Pius V (1566-1572) issued two Constitutions directly referring to Institutes in which only simple vows were taken. Three years after the conclusion of the Council of Trent he issued the first of these, in which he addressed himself to the reform of women religious.[16] Two years later he issued the Constitution *Lubricum vitæ genus,* which was concerned with Institutes of men in which simple vows were taken. The Pontiff declared that all those men who lived a common life under voluntary obedience without solemn vows and who wore a habit distinct from that of the secular priests were commanded, within twenty-four hours after receiving notice of the Constitution, to adopt one of the rules

[13] Cf. const. *Quanto fructuosius,* 1 febr. 1583 — *Codicis Iuris Canonici Fontes* (Cura Emi Petri Card. Gasparri editi, 9 vols., Romae postea Civitate Vaticana: Typis Polyglottis Vaticanis, 1923-1939), (Vols. VII-IX, ed. cura et studio Emi Iustiniani Card. Serédi), n. 150 (hereinafter cited as *Fontes*).

[14] Cf. *infra,* pp. 19,20,21.

[15] Stephanus Sipos, *Enchiridion Iuris Canonici* (Pécs, 1926), p. 316.

[16] Const. *Circa pastoralis,* 29 maii 1566 — *Fontes,* n. 112.

of religious approved by the Church, and within a month to receive solemn vows. Failure to comply with these instructions was to be punished, and superiors were threatened with deprivation of office, dignities, benefices, and even with excommunication, if they failed to carry out the provisions of the Constitution.[17] This Constitution seemed to have the effect of placing a total prohibition on Institutes of men in which only simple vows were taken and whose members wore habits distinct from that of the secular clergy, since it was addressed to the Canons of St. George and the Hermits of St. Jerome and all other Congregations of whatever type. The authors, however, are in dispute as to the extension of this law. Creusen states that its force remained doubtful.[18] Some held that it applied to all communities of men in simple vows.[19] Others denied that it was a universal prohibition.[20] The decree itself made no direct reference to future foundations of Institutes of simple vows, nor was there any mention made, as previously had been made in the Constitution regarding women religious,[21] of the invalidity of future professions made in Congregations which had received papal approval before the decree.

It is evident that Pope St. Pius V had very clear and definite views on Congregations of simple vows in which the members wore habits distinct from that of the secular clergy. He desired

---

[17] 17 nov. 1568 — *Bull. Rom Taur.*, VII, 725-726.

[18] Joseph Creusen, *De Iuridica Status Religiosi Evolutione* (2. ed., Romae: Apud Aedes Pontificae Universitatis Gregorianae, 1948), p. 34.

[19] Bizzarri, *Collectanea, p.* 213, 742 and footnote; A. P. Steiger, "De Propagatione et Diffusione Vitae Religiosae," *Periodica de Religiosis et Missionariis* (Brugis, 1905-1919; ab anno 1920: *Periodica de Re Canonica et Morali utilia praesertim Religiosis et Missionariis,* Brugis, 1920-1927; ab anno 1927: *Periodica de Re Morali, Canonica, Liturgica,* Brugis, 1927-1936, et Romae, 1937-   ), XIII (1924), (172) (hereinafter cited as *Periodica*).

[20] Cf. Arcadius Larraona, "Commentarium in Partem Secundum libri II Codicis, quae est: De Religiosis," *Commentarium pro Religiosis* (Romae, 1920-1934; ab anno 1935: *Commentarium pro Religiosis et Missionariis*), I (1920), 48, note (10) (this article hereinafter cited as "De Religiosis" and the periodical as *CpR* and *CpRM* respectively).

[21] Const. *Circa pastoralis,* 29 maii 1566 — *Fontes,* n. 112.

that they be suppressed and that they should not arise in the future. But shortly after his death (1572) there is evidence that a number of Congregations of men who took only simple vows were approved by the later Pontiffs. In many of the newly-founded Institutes, at first, only simple vows were taken, but at a later time, after permission was obtained from the Holy See, the members took solemn vows.[22] Other Institutes in which simple vows were taken received papal approval and the members of these Institutes continued to take simple vows.[23]

The prescriptions of Pope St. Pius V in his Constitution *Lubricum vitæ genus* were not strictly enforced, and it seems that the law fell into desuetude by reason of the numerous approba-

---

[22] E.g., the Congregation of Clerks Regular Administering to the Sick, Sixtus V, const. *Ex omnibus,* 18 mart. 1586 — *Bull. Rom. Taur.,* VIII, 669 sqq.; Clemens VIII, const. *Illius,* 21 sept. 1591 — *Bull. Rom. Taur.,* IX, 479-488; the Clerics Regular of the Mother of God, Clemens VIII, *Ex quo divina,* 13 oct. 1595 — *Bull. Rom. Taur.,* X, 227-229; Gregorius XV, *In supremo,* 3 nov. 1621 — *Bull. Rom. Taur.,* XII, 608-609; the Congregation of Christian Doctrine, Clemens VIII, const. *Exposcit debitum,* 23 dec. 1597 — *Bull. Rom. Taur.,* X, 411-413; Paulus V, const. *Ex iniuncto,* 11 apr. 1616 — *Bull. Rom. Taur.,* 353-356; the Poor Clerics of the Mother of God of the Pious Schools, Paulus V, const. *Ad ea,* 16 mart. 1617 — *Bull. Rom. Taur.,* XIII, 382-385; Gregorius XV, const. *In supremo,* 18 nov. 1621 — *Bull. Rom. Taur.,* XII, 627-628; the Clerics Regular of the Pious Schools, Gregorius XV, const. *In supremo,* 18 nov. 1621 — *Bull. Rom. Taur.,* XII, 627-628; the Confraternity of Bethlehemites, Innocentius XI, const. *Ecclesiae Catholicae,* 26 martii 1678 — *Bull. Rom. Taur.,* XIX, 735-751; Clemens XI, const. *Ex debito,* 3 apr. 1710 — *Bull. Rom. Taur.,* XXI, 385-387; the Confraternity of St. Hippolytus, Innocentius XII, const. *Ex debito,* 20 maii 1700 — *Bull. Rom. Taur.,* XX, 931; the Portugal Congregation of Discalced Monks of St. Paul the First Hermit, Pius VI, const. *Ex debito,* 3 febr. 1784 — *Bullarii Romani Continuatio Summorum Pontificum* (19 vols. in 20, Prati, 1835-1857), IX, 1337 (hereinafter cited as *Bull. Rom. Con.*); the Order of Friars of Penance, Pius VI, const. *Ex debito,* 21 maii 1784 — *Bull. Rom. Con.,* IX, 1381-1382; the Immaculate Conception Marianists, Pius VI, const. *Ex debito,* 27 mart. 1787 — *Bull. Rom. Con.,* IX, 1782-1795.

[23] E.g., the Congregation of the Most Holy Redeemer, Benedictus XIV, brev. *Ad pastoralis,* 25 febr. 1749 — *Bull. Rom. Taur.,* XVI, 67-69; the Congregation of the Passion, Clemens XVI, const. *Supremi apostolatus,* 16 dec. 1769 — *Bull. Rom. Con.,* VII, 73.

tions of simple vow Congregations. During the seventeenth century, the number of clerical Congregations of simple vows approved was not numerous,[24] but during the eighteenth century their number increased. During the nineteenth century there was even a greater increase. Many of the old Orders in the Church were suppressed, exiled or denied juridical existence under the anti-religious civil laws enacted after the French Revolution (1789-1799).[25] Suffering from these baneful effects, the Church found that some of the great charitable and educational works of the old Orders could now be undertaken by Congregations of men and women who professed only simple vows.[26] The former reluctance to approve such Institutes now changed to open approbation and commendation. The Holy See saw fit to issue decrees of commendation or approval for five Congregations from 1816 to 1820; for thirteen of them from 1820 to 1830; for eighteen from 1830 to 1840; for twenty-three from 1840 to 1850; for forty-two from 1850 to 1860; for three from 1860 to 1862, and for seventy-four from 1862 to 1865.[27]

Such was the phenomenal growth in the numbers of the new Congregations that with reference thereto in the agenda for the Vatican Council (1869-1870) a letter dated June 6, 1867, was addressed to all the bishops of the Church by Pope Pius IX (1846-1878). He asked whether the number of Congregations should be allowed to increase, or whether simply the already approved Institutes should be strengthened. However, before this question was discussed, the Council was forced to adjourn. The answer of the bishops of France is the only direct reply on

[24] Creusen, *De Iuridica Status Religiosi Evolutione*, p. 36.

[25] Creusen, *De Iuridica Status Religiosi Evolutione*, pp. 38-39; Charles Tyck, *Notices Historiques sur les Congrégations et Communautés Religieuses du XIXme Siècle* (Louvain, 1892), Appendix I, pp. 293-323 (hereinafter cited as *Notices Historiques*).

[26] Steiger, "De Propagatione et Diffusione Vitae Religiosae," *Periodica*, XIII (1924), (174)-(175).

[27] Tyck, *Notices Historiques*, Appendix III, p. 335.

record.[28] They answered that the number of such Congregations should be allowed to increase. The bishops of Holland and Belgium, by praising the newly-founded Congregations and stressing their utility, concurred indirectly in this opinion.[29]

The Sacred Congregation of Bishops and Regulars, after the Council of the Vatican, undertook the study of the problem of this remarkable growth in the number of Congregations. In order to guard against the danger of abuses as resulting from the multiplicity of new Congregations, a special commission was constituted within the Sacred Congregation of Bishops and Regulars. It was the function of this commission to deal with the approval of new Congregations.[30] When the Constitution *Conditæ a Christo* of Pope Leo XIII (1878-1903) was issued on December 8, 1900, there were incorporated in it many of the rules which had been followed by this commission of the Sacred Congregation of Bishops and Regulars.[31] In the year following the appearance of the Constitution *Conditæ a Christo,* the Sacred Congregation of Bishops and Regulars issued a set of instructions *(Normæ)* which gave in outline the required procedure for obtaining papal approbation for new Congregations.[32] These *Normæ,* which had no force of law, were later superseded by the *Normæ* issued in 1921.[33] The Constitution *Conditæ a Christo* referred to above and which has been styled the *Magna Charta* of simple vow Congregations,[34] gave these Congregations a truly juridic character and a place of honor in the written

---

28 Cf. *Acta et Decreta Sacrorum Conciliorum Recentiorum, Collectio Lacensis* (7 vols., Friburgi Brisgoviae, 1870-1892), VII, 1028, q. 10, 837a (hereinafter cited as *Collectio Lacensis*).

29 *Collectio Lacensis,* VII, 877a.

30 Albert Battandier, *Guide Canonique pour les Constitutions des Instituts à Voeux Simples* (6. ed., Paris, 1923), p. 7, n. 16.

31 *Fontes,* n. 644.

32 *Normae secundum quas S. Cong. Episcoporum et Regularium procedere solet in approbandis Novis Institutis Votorum Simplicium, 28 iunii 1901* (Romae: Typis S. Cong. de Propaganda Fide, 1901).

33 *Acta Apostolicae Sedis, Commentarium Officiale* (Romae, 1909-1929; Civitate Vaticana, 1929-   ), XIII (1921), 312-319 (hereinafter cited as *AAS*).

34 Larraona, "De Religiosis," *CpR,* I (1920), p. 117, n. 17.

legislation of the Church. No longer was it a question of definite and firm opposition to the very existence of such Congregations, nor was there mere toleration of them; the Institutes in which the members lived a common life and took simple vows were looked on with favor and full approbation, subject of course to the prudent rules and regulations which the Holy See had seen fit to enact in regard to their foundation and organization.

Article 2. The Law Governing the Newly-founded Congregations

A. The statement of the problem

One of the problems that resulted from the great multiplicity of newly-founded Congregations was concerned with the juridical government of these Institutes. By what rules and laws were they to be governed? Did the *Ius Regulare* apply to them? The *Ius Regulare* was that body of laws which had been enacted by the Councils of the Church and the Sovereign Pontiffs for Regulars, and which constituted the common law whereby Institutes of solemn vows were governed. If the *Ius Regulare* did apply to Congregations of simple vows, were any exceptions to be made? If it did not apply, what were the general laws for these new Congregations?

In the opinion of Nervegna († 1906), all regulations enacted by the Sovereign Pontiffs for the Orders of Regulars were to be applied in their entirety to Institutes of simple vows, exception being made for those things which were specifically declared by law as not applicable to Congregations of simple vows.[35] Nervegna stated that one of the principal reasons for maintaining this view was based on the Bull *Debitum pastoralis* of Pope Innocent XII (1691-1700), as issued on August 4, 1698. The Sovereign Pontiff had declared that faculties for the foundation and suppression of religious houses were to be obtained from the Sacred Congregation of Cardinals and Prelates for the Discipline of Regulars. He furthermore had demanded that the faculties to

[35] I. Nervegna, *De Institutis Votorum Simplicium Religiosorum et Monialium* (Romae, 1904), pp. 22-23.

invest novices with the habit and to receive their profession were to be obtained from the same Sacred Congregation. These prescriptions had been imposed by Pope Innocent XII on all monks and regulars of every Order, Congregation, Society and Institute, both mendicant and non-mendicant.[36] The Pope further had stated that his law applied to all men religious throughout the world.[37]

The use of this Bull, as Nervegna wished to use it, in order to support the opinion that the whole of the *Ius Regulare* was to be applied to Institutes of simple vows, apart from those cases in which the law provided specific exceptions, hardly seems justified. There was no mention in the Bull of Pope Innocent XII of the application of the whole body of laws governing Regulars to the Congregations of simple vows. To seek to show that Pope Innocent's Bull extended to matters other than those that received mention in the Bull seems to make the conclusion of the syllogism wider than the premises.

The solution of the problem concerning the laws governing Congregations of simple vows as outlined by Larraona seems to be a better one. There was no common law which unified the legislation for this great diversity of Congregations and which was accommodated to their needs.[38] It is true that, in approving the foundation of these new Congregations and in approving the Constitutions which had been submitted, the Holy See had set up particular laws to govern the individual Institutes. For example, there was no general legislation before the Code re-

[36] The writer has not been able to locate the text of this Bull in the sources which are available, but it is reprinted in Nervegna, *De Iure Practico Regularium* (Romae, 1900), pp. 9-16. The author stated that the text of this Bull was reprinted "juxta textum existentem apud Secretariam ad usum et regimen S. Congregationis super Disciplina Regulari." The date of the Bull is given as Aug. 12th in *De Institutis Votorum Simplicium Religiosorum et Monialium* (p. 23), and as Aug 4th, in the reprint of the text of the Bull in *De Iure Practico Regularium* (pp. 9-16).

[37] Cf. Nervegna, *De Iure Practico Regularium*, p. 12, n. 4; pp. 73-74.

[38] Larraona, "De Religiosis," *CpR*, I (1920), pp. 134 sqq.; nn. 14, 15, 16; cf. Sebastianus Sanguineti, *Iuris Ecclesiastici Privati Institutiones* (3. ed., Romae, 1896), p. 320.

garding the simple vow of poverty professed in Institutes which were either papally or episcopally approved as simple vow Congregations. The Institutes were guided in the matter of poverty by private legislation.[39] But there was, in fact, no common law by which all Institutes of simple vows were to be governed. The common law of the Regulars was not in itself applicable to Congregations, for in the first place the members of the Congregations were not Regulars. The laws governing solemn vows, the obligations of the papal cloister, and the privilege of exemption were not of themselves applicable to simple vow Institutes, since the members were not bound by solemn vows, nor by the obligation of the papal cloister, nor did they enjoy the privilege of exemption except by special indult. Furthermore, the ends or purposes of the foundation of these Congregations in many instances differed widely from the purposes of the foundation of the old Orders. The general laws of the latter were not accommodated to the needs of the former. Nor indeed could the body of laws governing the lay confraternities and third orders secular be applied to them.

The opinion of Larraona, which holds that before the promulgation of the Code there was no common law to govern Congregations of simple vows, seems to the present writer to have greater juridic support than the opposite opinion espoused by Nervegna. It will be the purpose of the second section of this article to show that the common law for Congregations was not fully formulated before the Code, but that steps were taken toward the establishment of a unified law. There will be cited a number of examples in which laws formerly enacted for Regulars were extended to Congregations. If, as Nervegna maintained, the *Ius Regulare* already applied to Congregations, what would have been the need for the Holy See to apply portions of this common law of Regulars to Congregations ? In addition to supporting the view concerning the lack of a common law for Congregations, the citations of the various instances of the application

[39] Sidney Turner, *The Vow of Poverty,* The Catholic University of America Studies in Canon Law, n. 54 (Washington, D.C.: The Catholic University of America, 1929), p. 90.

of the law of Regulars to Congregations will demonstrate the development of the legal thinking regarding these Institutes of simple vows.

B. The extension of the common law of Regulars to non-exempt Congregations

The Holy See recognized the need of formulating a unified system of laws which would be accommodated to the needs of these new Institutes. The great increase in the number of approved Congregations during the nineteenth century was helpful in bringing about a movement toward the unification of the laws governing Congregations. Some of the laws which had formerly applied to religious Orders were extended to the Congregations, and, in addition, there were issued by the Holy See some decrees which showed a tendency to revise some of the old laws which governed the ancient Orders and to bring into being laws which were to govern both the regular Orders and the Congregations.

As evidence of this tendency towards a unification, extension and revision of the legislation, a number of examples will be cited. These examples will deal with a wide variety of aspects of the religious life, e.g., entrance to the Institute, the novitiate, poverty, alms-gathering, the incurring of debts, confession and communion, testimonial letters for ordination, clerical studies, preaching, expulsion from the Institute and its effects. It is not claimed that these were the only points of harmony between the law for Regulars and the law for members of Congregations. But it must be remembered that each of the approved Congregations had its own set of approved Rules, Statutes or Constitutions, and that these various particular laws had incorporated many other features from the *Ius Regulare*. But in this treatise there is to be traced the growth of the general law for Congregations, not the particular law of each of them.

The examples are cited here in support of the opinion that, since the Holy See in these several instances applied the *Ius Regulare* to Congregations, it can be concluded that before the Code there was no common law for Congregations, but that the

Holy See, by virtue of these and other declarations, was moving toward the formulation of a common law for Congregations of simple vows.

In reply to questions proposed by the Oblates of Mary, the Sacred Congregations of Bishops and Regulars drew attention to the fact that Pope Benedict XIV (1740-1758) had legislated on the admission of the secular clergy into religious Orders, and had stated that the religious state offered greater security for spiritual health, and thus the bishops were not to impede those members of the secular clergy who wished to embrace the religious state.[40] The Sacred Congregation of Bishops and Regulars stated that the profession of simple vows in any approved Institute offered a similar security, and thus the reasoning of Pope Benedict applied to Institutes of simple vows. Hence the secular clergy were not to be impeded from entering such Institutes.[41] A similar reply was sent to the Bishop of Orleans,[42] and the reply cited above as given to the Oblates was used in the solution of a similar case.[43]

Several decrees and declarations issued by the Holy See harmonized the practices of Orders and Congregations with reference to the reasons for refusing to accept certain types of postulants into the Institute.[44]

Again it was declared that in each and every Order, Congregation, Society, Institute, Monastery, and House, whether solemn or simple vows were taken, there was the necessity of obtaining testimonial letters regarding those who desired to receive the habit. These letters were to be obtained from the ordinary of the diocese of origin and also from the ordinaries of the places where the aspirant had stayed for more than a year

---

[40] Litt. *Ex quo dilectus,* 14 ian. 1747 — *Fontes,* n. 374.

[41] S. C. Ep. et Reg., *Pinerolien.,* 28 iul. 1837, ad 2 — *Fontes,* n. 1914.

[42] S. C. Ep. et Reg., *Aurelianen.,* 20 dec. 1859 — *Fontes,* n. 1972.

[43] Bizzarri, *Collectanea,* p. 710.

[44] S. C. de Religiosis, decr. 7 sept. 1909 — *Fontes,* n. 4396; declar. 4 ian. 1910 — *Fontes,* n. 4399; declar. 5 apr. 1910 — *Fontes,* n. 4400; 3 iul. 1910 — *Fontes,* n. 4404.

after the time at which the person came to be fourteen years of age.[45] Further declarations were made on this same subject in the following years.[46]

While in the opinion of Bouix the laws which governed novitiates in solemn vow Institutes in general were not extended to Congregations of simple vows,[47] there were instances in which portions of the law of Regulars concerned with the novitiate were extended to Congregations. The legislation enacted by Pope Sixtus V (1585-1590), whereby children born of incestuous and sacrilegious unions were forbidden, under pain of invalidity, from receiving the habit or making profession in Regular Orders, was later applied to Congregations of simple vows.[48] Pope Clement VIII (1592-1605) had enacted legislation for Regular Orders regarding the novitiate house and its furnishings, the qualities required of the Novice Master and his *Socius,* and their obligations, and the spiritual exercises of the novices. This legislation was applied to Congregations of simple vows.[49] The decree *Regulari disciplinæ* reaffirmed the above-mentioned laws of Popes Sixtus V and Clement VIII and declared that these former decrees were thereupon to be observed in Institutes of solemn vows and also in Institutes of simple vows in Italy and the adjacent islands. In addition to this former legislation on novitiates, the decree *Regulari disciplinæ* enacted laws which had reference to the investigation to be made of each candidate who sought to receive the habit, and of each novice who wished to make his profession. A board of examiners, consisting of the Provincial and seven other priests of the Institute, or at least of three others

---

[45] S. C. super Statu Regularium, decr. *Romani Pontifices,* 25 ian. 1848 — *Fontes,* n. 4375.

[46] S. C. super Statu Regularium, declar. 1 maii 1851 — *Fontes,* n. 4377; 5 nov. 1852 — *Fontes,* n. 4380; 29 maii 1857 — *Fontes,* n. 4382.

[47] Bouix, 1, 577, n. 11.

[48] Cf. const. *Cum de omnibus,* 26 nov. 1587 — *Fontes,* n. 162; S. C. super Statu Regularium, decr. *Regulari disciplinae,* 25 ian. 1848 — *Fontes,* n. 4376.

[49] Cf. const. *Cum ad regularem,* 19 maii 1603 — *Fontes,* n. 189; S. C. super Statu Regularium, decr. *Regulari disciplinae,* 25 ian. 1848 — *Fontes,* n. 4376.

in smaller Institutes, was to investigate in detail the qualifications of the aspirants to membership in the Institute. The examination to be held before the admitting of the novice to profession was to establish the rectitude of his motives, and his freedom from force and fear in making his profession.[50] Further detail in the legislation on the novitiate is given in later declarations.[51]

The legislation on the vow of poverty was affected by the encyclical letter *Neminem latet* and subsequent declarations. They required that the novices in Orders of men, before being admitted to solemn vows, were to take simple vows for a three-year period. It was also declared that while the religious in Orders of men were bound by simple vows they were able to retain the *dominium radicale* of their goods.[52] This latter statement was in harmony with the legislation whereby religious in simple vow Institutes retained the *dominium radicale* of their goods.[53]

Regulations governing alms-gathering by non-mendicant Orders and Congregations were unified by a decree of the Sacred Congregation for Religious,[54] and a uniform law for Orders and Congregations regarding the incurring of debts and obligations by members of such Institutes was issued by the same Sacred Congregation.[55]

The Holy See moved to unify the discipline of the Church regarding the confession and communion of members of regular Orders and of simple vow Institutes. The former legislation

---

[50] S. C. super Statu Regularium, decr. *Regulari disciplinae,* 25 ian. 1848 — *Fontes,* n. 4376.

[51] S. C. super Statu Regularium, declar. 1 maii 1851 — *Fontes,* n. 4378; Bizzarri, *Collectanea,* pp. 850, 851.

[52] S. C. super Statu Regularium, 19 mart 1857 — *Fontes,* n. 4381; 12 iun. 1858 — *Fontes,* n. 4383, IX; Bizzarri, *Collectanea,* pp. 853-854, 856.

[53] Cf. S. C. Ep. et Reg., *Pinerolien.,* 28 iul. 1837 — *Fontes,* n. 1914; S. C. Ep. et Reg., *Trappensium,* 20 dec. 1861 — *Fontes,* n. 1982.

[54] S. C. de Religiosis, decr. 21 nov. 1908, pars II — *Fontes,* n. 4391; cf. S. C. Ep. et Reg., decr. *Singulari,* 27 mart. 1896, n. 2, 4 — *Fontes,* n. 2029.

[55] S. C. de Religiosis, instr. *Inter ea,* 30 iul. 1909 — *Fontes,* n. 4394; cf. *Fontes,* n. 4404.

regarding ordinary and extraordinary confessors which had been proper to Institutes of solemn vows[56] was extended, and thenceforth was to be observed by both Orders and Congregations alike.[57] Members of Institutes, whether of Orders or of Congregations, were granted the same liberty of choice of a confessor by virtue of the decrees of the Sacred Congregation for Religious.[58] And it was further stated that it was the confessor who was to regulate the reception of the Holy Eucharist by his penitent.[59] The superior was not to interfere in this matter except in cases of grave scandal.[60] Frequent and even daily Communion was to be fostered in all types of Institutes.[61]

In drawing up a new law to govern the granting of dimissorial letters for ordination, the Sacred Congregation of Bishops and Regulars cited some of the former legislation which had been proper to Regulars. By these former laws the superiors of regular Orders were forbidden to grant dimissorial letters to novices or to such as were professed with temporary vows, if they were to be promoted to sacred orders under the title of poverty.[62] These former laws, issued for solemn vow Institutes, were applied to Institutes in which simple vows were taken. It was further stated that the members of these Institutes were not to be promoted to sacred orders under the title *mensæ communis* or *missionis* unless they had taken simple perpetual vows or were otherwise joined *stabiliter* to the Institute.[63]

---

56 Conc. Trident., sess. XXV, *de regularibus,* c. 10; Benedictus XIV, const. *Pastoralis curae,* 5 aug. 1748 — *Fontes,* n. 388.

57 S. C. Ep. et Reg., decr. *Quemadmodum,* 17 dec. 1890 — *Fontes,* n. 2017.

58 S. C. de Religiosis, *Cum de sacramentalibus,* 3 febr. 1913 — *AAS,* V (1913), 62-64; decr. *In audientia,* 5 aug. 1913 — *AAS,* V (1913), 431.

59 S. C. Ep. et Reg., litt. 4 aug. 1888 — *Fontes,* n. 2013.

60 S. C. Ep. et Reg., decr. *Quemadmodum,* 17 dec. 1890 — *Fontes,* n. 2017.

61 S. C. C., decr. *Sacra Tridentina Synodus,* 20 dec. 1905 — *Fontes,* n. 4326, nn. 7, 8; cf. *Fontes,* n. 4404.

62 Pius V, const. *Romanus Pontifex,* 14 oct. 1568 — *Fontes,* n. 129; cf. S. C. super Statu Regularium, declar. 12 iun. 1858 — *Fontes,* n. 4383.

63 S. C. Ep. et Reg., decr. *Auctis admodum,* 4 nov. 1892 — *Fontes,* n. 2020.

Those who were professed, whether with solemn or with simple vows, were governed by a uniform law also on the question of the curriculum of studies in preparation for the reception of sacred orders.[64]

In unifying some of the legislation on public preaching, the Sacred Congregation of Bishops and Regulars drew attention to previous prescriptions made by the Council of Trent on this point.[65] The Sacred Congregation then forbade the members of both Orders and Congregations from preaching in public without the knowledge of the local bishop.[66]

The tendency toward harmonizing the legislation for Orders and Congregations was also evident in connection with the legislation governing the canonical process of expulsion from the Institute. Once more in its decree the Sacred Congregation drew attention to the previous legislation issued for solemn vow Institutes by specifically referring to the previous laws on expulsion.[67] The decree *Auctis admodum* stated that this previous legislation not only remained in force, but was to be extended and imposed on superiors of Institutes of simple vows.[68] Those in sacred orders, by virtue of this same decree *Auctis admodum,* whether they were members of Institutes of solemn or of simple vows, were upon their dismissal from the Institute to remain under perpetual suspension until the Holy See made further provision.[69]

While it is true, as shown by the documents cited above, that a great portion of the *Ius Regulare* was applied to simple

[64] S. C. Ep. et Reg., decr. *Auctis admodum,* 4 nov. 1892 — *Fontes,* n. 2020, n. 6; cf. S. C. de Religiosis, declar. 7 sept. 1909 — *Fontes,* n. 4397; declar. 21 dec. 1909 — *Fontes,* n. 4398.

[65] Conc. Trident., sess. V, *de ref.,* c. 2.

[66] S. C. Ep. et Reg., instr. 31 iul. 1864, n. 7 — *Fontes,* n. 2024.

[67] S. C. C., decr. *Sacra Congregatio,* 21 sept. 1624 — *Bull. Rom. Taur.,* V, 248-250; S. C. C., decr. *Instantibus,* 24 iul. 1694 — *Fontes,* n. 2942.

[68] S. C. Ep. et Reg., decr. *Auctis admodum,* 4 nov. 1892: "... nedum in se robore manent, sed servandae imponuntur etiam superioribus Institutorum votorum simplicium." — *Fontes,* n. 2020.

[69] *Fontes,* n. 2020; cf. S. C. Ep. et Reg., *Abulen.,* 20 nov. 1895 — *Fontes,* n. 2026; S. C. de Religiosis, 1 sept. 1912 — *Fontes,* n. 4415.

vow Congregations, there are instances in which the Holy See declared that the *Ius Regulare* did not apply to Congregations. Three examples of this may be cited.

Profession in a simple vow Institute did not entail the loss of simple benefices, although such a profession did entail the loss of residential benefices.[70] The profession of Regulars according to the *Ius Regulare,* involved the loss of even simple benefices.[71]

It was also declared that the Oblates of Mary were not bound to observe the law enacted by the Council of Trent for Regulars regarding processions.[72] Though this declaration was addressed to one Congregation, it was considered as applying to all other Congregations.[73]

There is another example of a decree issued by the Holy See whereby the law of Regulars was declared as not applicable to Institutes of simple vows. It emanated from the Sacred Penitentiary. By virtue of this declaration, the members of Congregations of simple vows were not bound by the prohibition imposed on Regulars to refrain from bestowing gifts.[74]

It was from the collection of such decrees, a few of which have been cited above, that the legislation governing Congregations was developed. As Cardinal Gasquet (1846-1929) stated in the Introduction he wrote for the third volume of Augustine's *Commentary on the New Code of Canon Law,* "Hitherto [i.e., before the promulgation of the Code], legislation in regard to religious had been in what may be called 'a fluid state.' It was mostly based upon special Pontifical Constitutions and deductions from the same, and had not hitherto been gathered together and

---

[70] S. C. Ep. et Reg., *Pinerolien.*, 28 iul. 1837, ad 2 — *Fontes,* n. 1914; cf. 25 aug. 1903 — *Fontes,* n. 2045.

[71] Cf. c. 4, *de regularibus et transeuntibus ad religionem,* III, 14, in VI°; Benedictus XIV, ep. *Ex quo,* 14 ian. 1747 — *Fontes,* n. 374.

[72] *Fontes,* n. 1914; cf. Conc. Trident., sess. XXV, *de regularibus,* c. 13.

[73] Cf. Bizzarri, *Collectanea,* pp. 430, 432.

[74] S. Poenitentiaria, 15 mart. 1861, ad 2um — cf. F. Piat (Jean Joseph Loiseaux), *Praelectiones Iuris Regularis* (2. ed., Tornaci, 1896-1898), p. 263, e).

coordinated officially. The marvellous growth of religious bodies and the variety, especially in modern times, of their scope and purpose had rendered it difficult, to say the least, to set out the ecclesiastical law applicable to them." [75]

Some of the decrees which were issued by the Holy See were of a specific character and they were directed to one or the other of the various Congregations. It was by arguing from this specific legislation and by extending it by way of analogy to other Congregations in similar situations that a goodly portion of the legislation proper to Congregations was developed, even though this extension of a specific law for a common application seemed at times to be rather arbitrary.[76]

With the issuance of the Constitution *Conditæ a Christo* on December 8, 1900,[77] the juridic character of Congregations, whether of papal or of diocesan approval, was accurately defined. The *Normæ* of June 28, 1901, not only outlined the mode of procedure in the seeking of approval for Congregations, but collected in a unified body all the laws which referred to the internal rule of Congregations.[78]

With the publication of the Constitution *Conditæ a Christo* and the *Normæ,* a notable step toward the formulation of the common law for Congregations had been achieved. It remained only for the Code of Canon Law itself to perfect and supplement the previous legislation which governed simple vow Congregations.

---

[75] Charles Augustine, *A Commentary on the New Code of Canon Law* (8 vols., Vol. II, 3. ed., 1919; Vol. III, 4. ed., 1929; St. Louis: B. Herder Book Co.), III, Introduction (hereinafter cited as *Commentary*).

[76] Cf. Larraona, "De Religiosis," *CpR,* I (1920), p. 136, n. 16, a).

[77] *Fontes,* n. 644.

[78] Cf. Larraona, "De Religiosis," *CpR,* I (1920), 171-172.

PART II

CANONICAL COMMENTARY

CHAPTER II

THE OFFICE OF A LOCAL SUPERIOR IN A NON-EXEMPT CLERICAL CONGREGATION

Since the local superior in a non-exempt clerical Congregation is the head of a subordinate and imperfect society, it is necessary to examine precisely what his position is as head of such a society.

A society may be defined as a union of a number of men using common means to attain the same end.[1] This union is not one based merely on space or time such as exists in a group of men gathered together in a room, but it is a union in which the intellects and wills of the individual members are linked together by a moral bond.[2] Each member knows the end for which the society exists, and each, along with his fellow members, exercises his will to strive for the common goal. In a well organized society, all the members are of one mind and one will. Without such a bond of union there would be little more than a physical conglomeration of individuals which would be ill suited to attain a common end.[3]

The end of a society is of paramount importance in determining the nature and juridic status of the society. Societies are specified and distinguished one from another by their ends. Thus a society will be termed necessary, subordinate, perfect, imperfect, or spiritual, in as much as its end is necessary, subordinate, perfect, imperfect, or spiritual.[4] The end of the society

---

1 Alaphridus Ottaviani, *Institutiones Iuris Publici Ecclesiastici* (3. ed., 2 vols., Civitate Vaticana: Typis Polyglottis Vaticana, 1947), I, 33 (hereinafter cited as *Institutiones*); Udalricus Beste, *Introductio in Codicem* (3. ed., Collegeville, Minn.: St. John's Abbey Press, 1946), p. 38; Felix Cappello, *Summa Iuris Publici Ecclesiastici* (2. ed., Romae: apud aedes Universitatis Gregorianae, 1928), p. 36.

2 Ottaviani, *Institutiones*, I, 35-37; Cappello, *Summa Iuris Publici Ecclesiastici*, p. 37, nota 4.

3 Beste, *Introductio in Codicem*, p. 38.

4 Cappello, *Summa Iuris Publici Ecclesiastici*, p. 38; Beste, *Introductio in Codicem*, p. 39.

may further be called the first principle or cause of the union, since it is precisely to attain the end of the society that the members band themselves together.[5]

A society is said to be perfect when it seeks a goal common to all men, and when the means necessary to attain that end are possessed by the society. Thus a perfect society is self-sufficient, independent, and autonomous, and its end is not ordained to the attainment of a higher good.[6] There are but two perfect societies: the Church and the State. The former seeks the ultimate good in the spiritual order; the latter, in the temporal order.[7] All other societies are imperfect.[8] The end of an imperfect society is an incomplete good, and such a society is itself ordained to the end of some higher society. For this reason, all imperfect societies are dependent on and ordained to either the Church or the State.[9]

From the outline thus far given, it can be seen that a non-exempt Congregation is truly a society, since it fulfills all the notes contained in the definition of a society. The Code itself defines a non-exempt Congregation as: a society approved by legitimate ecclesiastical authority, the members of which, in accordance with its laws, take public simple vows, either perpetual or temporary, and through these means tend to evangelical perfection.[10] Furthermore, since the end of a non-exempt Congregation is subordinated and ordained to the end of the Church as a whole, the Congregation is rightly styled an imperfect society.[11]

A consideration of the bond of union uniting the members of a non-exempt Congregation indicates that the Congregation is

---

5 Ottaviani, *Institutiones,* I, 42, n. 21.

6 Cappello, *Summa Iuris Publici Ecclesiastici,* p. 44, n. 41.

7 Beste, *Introductio in Codicem,* p. 41; Cappello, *Summa Iuris Publici Ecclesiastici,* p. 47, n. 43, 3°.

8 Cappello, *Summa Iuris Publici Ecclesiastici,* pp. 47-48, n. 43, 4°.

9 Ottaviani, *Institutiones,* I, 59.

10 Can. 488, 1°, 2°.

11 Timotheus Schaefer, *De Religiosis* (4. ed., Roma: Editrice "Apostolato Cattolico," 1947), p. 62, nota 86.

a juridic society and may be further qualified as being a voluntary organization. Societies are juridic in character if the members are bound to the society by a legal bond. If such a bond is lacking and if the members unite merely to attain some end without undertaking any juridic obligations, the resulting society is said to be amicable in character.[12] Examples of such amicable societies are musical, artistic and athletic societies. The religious Congregation is evidently juridic in character, since the definition of a Congregation as given by the Code states that the members of such a society bind themselves by public simple vows to strive after evangelical perfection.[13]

Juridic societies are subdivided into necessary and voluntary societies. A society is termed necessary when the end of the society is necessary in the sense that all men are bound to seek the end of the society and are bound to seek it along with other men in a social organization. There are two naturally necessary societies to which all men belong: the family and the State. The Church is a supernaturally necessary juridic society inasmuch as men must seek their supernatural end, and they do so in union with other men.[14]

A voluntary juridic society is one in which the members of their own free will assume obligations consistent with the attainment of the end of the society. One is free to join or refrain from joining such a society. If the voluntary society is what is called purely voluntary, the whole society is dependent on the will of the members. The origin of the society, its end, its form of organization, its constitutions, all these depend on the free will of the members. They are free to disassociate themselves from the society and can even dissolve the society if they so desire.[15]

There is, however, another type of voluntary society which is not purely voluntary. An individual is at liberty to associate

---

[12] Ottaviani, *Institutiones,* I, 44, n. 22.

[13] Can. 488, 1°, 2°.

[14] Ottaviani, *Institutiones,* I, 43-45.

[15] Cappello, *Summa Iuris Publici Ecclesiastici,* p. 41; Beste, *Introductio in Codicem,* p. 39; Ottaviani, *Institutiones,* I, 70.

himself with such a society but is not obliged to do so. However, once he has become a member he assumes obligations imposed by a higher authority for the common good, with the result that the end of the society, its form of organization and its constitutions no longer fall under the complete control of the members. The State, for example, could add certain rights, privileges and obligations to commercial societies existing in the State. This action would be prompted by the realization that such commercial organizations, even though they are voluntary societies, are intimately connected with the welfare of the State. The common good demands that such societies be partially regulated by the supreme society of which they are a part. The end of the imperfect commercial society is both subordinate and ordained to the supreme end of the perfect society, the State. It follows then that the State can regulate its subordinate societies so that the common good is not impaired.

In a similar manner, the Church can regulate the activities of its subordinate societies so that the common supernatural good which is the end of the Church may be the more easily attained. Thus the Church can impose obligations and confer rights on its subordinate societies.[16] The religious Congregation is a voluntary society in the sense that an individual is free to join it. But once he has assumed the juridic obligations of membership he cannot, because of the action of the higher authority, freely disassociate himself from the society, nor can he, along with the other members, dissolve the society,[17] nor can he change its end or constitutions.[18]

When two societies are compared one with the other, a further subdivision results. These societies are said to be on a par with each other *(societates pares)* if the end of each is of the same order and perfection. Thus, two religious Congregations, two pious unions or sodalities, are societies on a par with

---

16 Ottaviani, *Institutiones,* I, 70, nota 15.

17 Can. 493.

18 Matthaeus Conte a Coronata, *Institutiones Iuris Canonici ad Usum Utriusque Cleri et Scholarum* (5 vols., Vol. I and Vol. II, 2. ed., Taurini: Marietti, 1939), I, 649, n. 535, 3° (hereinafter cited as *Institutiones*).

each other.[19] However, if the end of one society is in a different and inferior order from that of the other, these two societies are not on a par with each other *(societates impares)*. This is the case when a society of the natural order is compared with one of the supernatural order.[20]

Even if the ends of the two societies compared are in the same order of perfection, a lack of parity may result from the fact that the end of one is subordinate, and ordained to that of the other. Thus, the end of the society known as the religious Congregation is of the same order of perfection as the end of the society known as the religious house or community. But since the religious house is subordinate, and ordained to the whole Congregation, these two societies are said to lack parity.[21]

Two religious houses or communities in the same religious Institute are societies on a par with each other, but since each of them operates independently of the other, each house is said to be a co-ordinate society.[22]

Thus, not only is the religious Institute, as a whole, to be considered as an imperfect voluntary society, but each community that is canonically erected as an independent house is also an imperfect voluntary society.

As noted above, in every society there must be a union of intellects and wills on the part of the members seeking to attain the common end of the society. However, when we consider man as he is, we find that his will tends to be inconstant and variable. He sets out to achieve a certain end, but oftentimes minor setbacks or difficulties deter him from this end. In order to counteract such tendencies and in order to assure the continued harmonious co-operation of all the members, there must be present in every society a certain authority whereby the members may be guided to the end of the society, and the wills of the individual members may be encouraged, or even coerced, into

---

19 Cappello, *Summa Iuris Publici Ecclesiastici,* p. 42, 7°.

20 Ottaviani, *Institutiones,* I, 49-50.

21 Ottaviani, *Institutiones,* I, 50, nota 38.

22 Cappello, *Summa Iuris Publici Ecclesiastici,* pp. 42-43, 8°; Ottaviani, *Institutiones,* I, 51.

seeking the good of the society.[23] This authority is so necessary, so inherently connected with the notion of the society, that it is impossible to have a true society without authority. Pope Leo XIII in his Encyclical *Immortale Dei* succinctly expressed this notion: "But as no society can hold together unless some one be over all, directing all to strive earnestly for the common good, every civilized community must have a ruling authority . . ."[24]

The authority inherent in the various types of societies varies according to the nature of the society in which it is exercised.[25] If it is granted that a literary society is a real society, then there is real authority in that society, although it obviously differs from the authority in a religious society. Authority in any society is to be exercised in accord with the end of the society and in conformity with the constitutions of the society. The members of a literary society, for example, could not be required to perform religious functions which clearly exceed the end and nature of their society. Even when the authority in the society urges the fulfillment of the ends of the literary society, the members are free to liberate themselves from that authority by leaving the society. The authority in a religious society, on the other hand, can require members to perform religious actions, since these actions clearly fall within the purview of the end of the religious society. Furthermore, the members of a religious society who have juridically bound themselves to this authority cannot liberate themselves from it at will. Thus, whether the society be purely amicable, juridic, necessary, voluntary, perfect

---

[23] Beste, *Introductio in Codicem,* pp. 38-39; Cappello, *Summa Iuris Publici Ecclesiastici,* p. 39; Ottaviani, *Institutiones,* I, 37, 65.

[24] 1 nov. 1885, n. 2 — *Fontes,* n. 592. Translation given in the text is taken from "Encyclical of Pope Leo XIII, The Christian Constitution of States," New York, N.Y.: The Paulist Press, 1941.

[25] Larraona, "De Potestate Dominativa Publica in Iure Canonico," *Acta Congressus Iuridici Internationalis Romae,* 12-17 Novembris, 1934 (5 vols., Romae: Apud Custodiam Librariam Pont. Instituti Utriusque Iuris, 1935-1937), IV, 148-149 (hereinafter the Acts of this Congress will be cited as *ACII,* and the article as "De Potestate Dominativa Publica").

or imperfect, there is authority in each of these societies, even though the authority in the various societies differs in measure and character depending on the nature of the society in which it is exercised.

The authority or power of ruling a perfect society, whether it be the Church or the State, is called public jurisdiction. The authority of the Church is called public ecclesiastical jurisdiction, and in virtue of it the members of the Church are authoritatively ruled and directed with regard to faith and morals.[26] The authority possessed by any imperfect society is generally called dominative power,[27] although other names are sometimes applied to this authority. Thus the authority of a father over his family (a naturally necessary imperfect society) is called domestic power.[28] The terms social[29] and economic[30] also serve to describe the authority inherent in an imperfect society.

As mentioned previously, the authority in various societies varies according to the nature and end of the society in which it is exercised. In the next chapter of this work the nature and extent of the authority possessed by the head of a religious imperfect society will be studied.

The authority in any society resides in the head of that group, whether the head be an individual or a group of individuals.[31] The method of selecting the head of the society varies

---

26 Beste, *Introductio in Codicem,* p. 215.

27 Albertus Blat, "De Potestate Superiorum in Religionibus Secundum Codicem I. C.," *CpRM,* XVI (1935), 325; Gordian Lewis, *Chapters in Religious Institutes,* The Catholic University of America Canon Law Studies, n. 181 (Washington, D.C.: The Catholic University of America Press, 1943), p. 51.

28 Arthurus Vermeersch-Josephus Creusen, *Epitome Iuris Canonici* (3 vols., Vol. I, 7. ed., Mechliniae-Romae: H. Dessain, 1949, Vol. III, 6. ed., Mechliniae-Romae: H. Dessain, 1946), I, 458, n. 619 (hereinafter cited as *Epitome*).

29 J. Biederlack-M. Führich, *De Religiosis* (Oeniponte: Rauch, 1919), pp. 54-55, n. 36.

30 Beste, *Introductio in Codicem,* p. 215.

31 Cappello, *Summa Iuris Publici Ecclesiastici,* p. 51, nn. 3, 4.

from one society to the next. Sometimes the members hold an election in order to choose a leader. In other societies the head of the society is appointed by higher superiors. In any event, as Pope Leo XIII noted, it is necessary in every society that there be a ruler over the members of the society, and that this ruler possess authority over the members.[32]

Having set forth the foregoing considerations on the notion of a society and on some of its subdivisions, the writer can next proceed to investigate the position held by a local superior in a non-exempt Congregation.

Article 1. The Office of Local Superior Considered in Itself

In religious Institutes, the authority to rule the members is exercised by superiors and chapters in conformity with the Constitutions of the Institutes or with the Code of Canon Law.[33]

The term "religious superior" is a generic term. It refers to those who possess at least dominative power over their subjects, and who in virtue of this power rule over either a religious house, or a province, or an Institute.[34] However, the superior's councillors, or his aides, such as the bursar and others who assist the superior in his task of ruling, are not termed superiors, but rather, officials.[35]

The two main classes of religious superiors indicated by the Code are major and minor superiors. This latter term, minor superior, is considered equivalent to the term local superior.[36]

---

[32] Ep. encycl. *Immortale Dei* — *Fontes,* n. 592.

[33] Can. 501, § 1.

[34] Schaefer, *De Religiosis,* p. 191, n. 426; Vermeersch-Creusen, *Epitome,* I, 457, n. 617; Hilaire Balmes, *Les Religieux à voeux simples d'après le Code* (Paray-le-Monial: Au Secrétariat des Oeuvres du Sacré-Coeur, 1921), p. 58; Coronata, *Institutiones,* I, 650, n. 536; Beste, *Introductio in Codicem,* p. 331.

[35] Beste, *Introductio in Codicem,* p. 331; Balmes, *Les Religieux à voeux simples d'après le Code,* p. 58; Vermeersch-Creusen, *Epitome,* I, 457, n. 617.

[36] Cf. can. 505; Index analytico-alphabeticus Codicis, s.v. *superiores;* Schaefer, *De Religiosis,* p. 193.

As the name indicates, a local superior is one whose authority is limited to one place. He is entrusted with the responsibility of ruling a single religious house. Whether the religious house be a *domus formata,* i.e., a house completely organized, or a *domus non formata,* i.e., a house but partially organized, the head of such a community is called the local superior, provided it is canonically erected as an independent religious house. Furthermore, the superiors or directors of schools, hospitals, and other houses devoted to pious works, are also to be considered superiors if they possess dominative power and have other religious under their authority with regard to religious discipline.[37] However, the case of a "filial house" is different. A filial house does not possess its own distinct moral personality, but is united to the principal house. It is entirely dependent on it, and is governed by one who is appointed by the superior who governs the whole community and resides in the principal house. The Sacred Congregation for Religious was asked whether the superiors of such strictly filial houses are to be included under the designation of local superiors in the Code. In reply, the Sacred Congregation stated that they were not to be so included.[38]

The growth and extension of religious Institutes gives rise to the necessity of dividing these Institutes into smaller units, so that each unit can be more effectively administered. It would be clearly impossible for the supreme head of a religious Institute to care personally for the needs of his subjects scattered throughout the world. Thus, the Institute is oftentimes divided into large units known as provinces, each of which is presided over by a provincial, who is called a major superior.[39] Each province in turn is composed of a number of individual religious houses.[40]

---

[37] Cf. *Pontificia Commissio ad Codicis Canones authentice Interpretandos,* 2-3 iun. 1918 — *AAS,* X (1918), 344 (hereinafter the replies of this Commission will be referred to with the abbreviation *PCI);* T. Lincoln Bouscaren, *The Canon Law Digest* (2 vols. and Supplement through 1948, Milwaukee: The Bruce Publishing Co., 1934, 1943, 1949), I, 275.

[38] 1 febr. 1924 — *AAS,* XVI (1924), 95; Bouscaren, *The Canon Law Digest,* I, 278.

[39] Can. 488, 8°.

[40] Can. 488, 6°.

Each of these houses is presided over and ruled by a local superior, who is in a better position to pay personal attention to the needs of the individual religious.

Since the local superior's office places him as head over a community which is an imperfect society, he rules his subjects by virtue of the authority which is possessed by the head of such an imperfect society. In fact, according to the teaching of Suarez,[41] following the doctrine of St. Thomas,[42] a superior is constituted solely in virtue of the power which belongs to him. In setting forth his doctrine on the virtue of obedience Suarez stated that the proximate object of that virtue is the precept or command of the superior. Obedience is due to the superior, not because he is a friend, not because he is a prudent man, but precisely because he occupies the office of superior. He is constituted a superior by virtue of his authority, otherwise all men would be equal to one another. Thus, Suarez concluded, obedience must be paid to the superior because he has authority.[43]

The office of the local superior in a non-exempt Congregation cannot be said to be an ecclesiastical office in the strict sense of the term, since neither the power of Orders nor that of jurisdiction is attached to it. However, it is an ecclesiastical office in the wide sense, since it is legitimately exercised for a spiritual end.[44]

Before concluding this article on the office considered in itself, the writer will indicate the general obligations attaching to the office.[45] Entrusted as he is with the care of a number of

[41] Suarez, *Omnia Opera, De Religione,* Tr. X, lib. IV, c. 14, n. 14 — Vol. XVI, pt. 2, 773.

[42] St. Thomas, *Doctoris Angelici Opera Omnia,* secundum impressionem Petri Fiaccadori Parmae 1852-1873 (photolithographice reimpressa), 25 vols., Vols. I-IV, *Summa Theologica,* New York: Musurga Publishers, 1948), *Summa Theologica,* IIa IIae, q. 104, art. 2 (hereinafter cited as *Summa Theologica*).

[43] Chapter III of this dissertation will discuss in greater detail the nature and extent of the local superior's authority.

[44] Can. 145.

[45] In Chapter V of this work a more detailed investigation will be made into the obligations attached to the office of local superior.

subjects, the local superior has the duty of looking out for the spiritual welfare of each of his subjects. With not only the Constitutions of his Institute but also the Code of Canon Law as a guide, the local superior is to direct his subjects in their quest for that spiritual perfection which is the goal of the religious life. He will have to study and be familiar with the letter and spirit of the Constitutions of his Institute, and he must further be fully conversant with the Church's law, especially regarding religious. His position of pre-eminence further demands that he set an example of religious regularity for his subjects.

Not only must the superior care for his subjects, but he must further provide for the prudent administration of the material goods of the community. Even though a local procurator or bursar is appointed to aid the superior in these matters,[46] the general obligation of supervising the administration of the goods of his community rests with the local superior.

An integral part of a religious Institute has been entrusted to the care of the local superior. It is his obligation to promote the spiritual and temporal welfare of that community.

Article 2. The Office of Local Superior Considered in Relation to the Office of Other Superiors in the Institute

Canon 502 states that the Superior General of any Institute has authority over all the provinces, the houses, and the members of the Institute. He must, however, exercise this authority according to the Constitutions. Other superiors have authority within the limits of their charge. In the greater number of present day religious Institutes there are three levels of authority: that of the Superior General; that of the provincial; and that of the local superior.[47] Such a hierarchy of authority implies a corresponding subjection. The local superior is immediately responsible to his provincial, and the provincial is responsible to the Superior General. Since, however, the local superior is

[46] Can. 516, § 2.

[47] Cf. Edward Heston, "Some Aspects of Government in Religious Communities," *The Jurist* (Washington, D.C., 1941-), X (1950), 36.

subject both to the provincial and the Superior General, he must endeavor to carry out in his house the directives which have been issued by the provincial and the Superior General. It is supposed, of course, that such directives have been issued in conformity to the common law and the Constitutions of the Institute. Thus, not only must the local superior aim for the good of his own community, but he must work for the spiritual and temporal welfare of the province and of the whole Institute.

While it is true that the local superior is subject to the vigilance and correction of higher superiors,[48] nevertheless the local superior is not merely an agent or delegate of his major superiors.[49] The Code itself confers authority on the local superior, and hence it is not the major superior who grants or delegates the authority by which the local superior rules his community. The Constitutions of various Congregations determine how the major superiors select those who are to rule the individual houses of the province, but the appointee does not become the vicar or delegate of his superior. He receives by law, in his own name, the authority necessary for the proper discharge of his duties as local superior.

When it speaks of the rights and obligations of religious superiors, the Code sometimes uses the word "superior" without qualifying it as referring either to major or minor superiors.[50] In such instances, any superior is to be understood as competent to act, unless the context of the law or the nature of the case indicates that the major superior, to the exclusion of the local superior, is indicated.[51] Thus, for example, the Code speaks in canon 514, § 1, of the right and duty of superiors to administer Viaticum and Extreme Unction to the novices and professed members of their communities as well as to the guests who reside in the house. The term "superiors" certainly includes the local

---

48 Goyeneche, "Consultationes," *CpRM,* XXII (1941), 24-25.

49 Heston, "Some Aspects of Government in Religious Communities," *The Jurist,* X (1950), 37.

50 Cf. cans. 454, § 5; 465, § 4; 514, § 1; 604, § 1; 609, § 3.

51 Schaefer, *De Religiosis,* p. 193, n. 429.

superior, since the law makes no distinction.[52] Similarly, permission to enter the cloister of a house of non-exempt religious can be granted by superiors.[53] Under this term "superiors" is to be included the local superior for the same reason as given in the first example.[54]

In order, however, to determine whether the local superior is to be considered as the religious superior empowered by the Code to remove religious pastors,[55] one must determine whether the local superior had the right to present his subject to the local ordinary as a candidate for the office of pastor. If the Constitutions of the Institute, using the liberty granted by the Code,[56] have conferred this right of presentation on the local superior, then it should follow that he can remove his subject from the office of pastor, after advising the local ordinary.[57] Generally, however, the Constitutions reserve this right of presentation to the major superior.[58] If the local superior lacks the right of presentation, he cannot remove a religious pastor who has been presented by a higher superior.

In certain instances the Code states that the Constitutions are to be consulted when one needs to determine whether the major or the minor superior is competent.[59] When the Constitutions contain such a designation, they are to be followed. However, if the Code leaves the specification to the Constitutions and no specification is made by them, the competent superior in such cases will be determined in the light of and with relation to the nature of the right or obligation concerned. If the matter clearly pertains to the Institute as a whole, or to the province as such, and not specifically to the welfare of the individual

---

[52] Schaefer, *De Religiosis,* p. 286, n. 566; Larraona, "Commentarium Codicis," *CpR,* IX (1928), 104, (c).

[53] Can. 604, § 1.

[54] Schaefer, *De Religiosis,* p. 706, n. 1188.

[55] Can. 454, § 5.

[56] Can. 456.

[57] Clancy, *The Local Religious Superior,* p. 109.

[58] Augustine, *Commentary,* II, 526.

[59] Cf. cans. 456; 561, § 1; 571, § 1; 572, § 6; 1228, § 2.

community, the superior indicated in such case will be a major superior. If, however, the matter concerns the welfare of an individual community, the local superior will enjoy the right or be subject to the obligation in question.[60] Thus the Code allows the Constitutions of the Institute to determine which superior shall be competent to dismiss novices.[61] If no such specification is made, the major superior, to the exclusion of the local superior, should be considered as being competent. This conclusion is drawn from a comparison of canon 571, § 1, with canon 543. Canon 543 reserves the right of admitting individuals to the novitiate and subsequent profession to the major superior with the vote of his council or of his chapter. It seems to follow, therefore, that the major superior alone is competent to dismiss novices.[62]

Having set forth the general nature of the office of local superior considered in itself and in relation to the office of other superiors, the writer proposes in the following chapter to investigate the nature of the authority attached to the office of the local superior.

---

[60] Cf. Servus Goyeneche, "Consultationes," *CpR,* III (1922), 217-219; E. Jombart, "Subordination dans l'Exercise de l'Authorité," *Révue des Communautés Religieuses* (Enghien, Belgique, 1925-), XI (1935), 69-75.

[61] Can. 571, § 1.

[62] Schaefer, *De Religiosis,* p. 531, n. 932; Romaeus William O'Brien, *The Provincial Religious Superior,* The Catholic University of America Canon Law Studies, n. 258 (Washington, D.C.: The Catholic University of America Press, 1947), pp. 92-93.

CHAPTER III

The Authority of the Local Superior

Article 1. The Definition and Nature of Dominative Power

The authority of the local superior in a non-exempt clerical Congregation is set forth early in the tract *"De Religiosis."* Canon 501, § 1, states that such a superior enjoys dominative power over his subjects in accord with the common law and the Constitutions of the Institute. The local superior does not possess ecclesiastical jurisdiction, since the same canon reserves such power to the superiors and chapters of exempt clerical Institutes.

The name "dominative" when applied to the authority of the religious superior over his subjects is derived from the relationship in Roman Law between the master *(dominus)* and his slave. St. Thomas Aquinas used the term dominative power to describe the power possessed by the lord over his servant.[1] Aristotle, to whom St. Thomas referred, had differentiated between the authority of the master with reference to his slave, and the authority of the father with reference to his son. St. Thomas called the master's authority dominative.[2] While St. Thomas seems not to have used the term dominative power in reference to the authority of the religious superior over his subjects, canonists and moralists who followed him used the term in this sense. It was commonly accepted that the relationship between the religious superior and his subject was very similar to the relationship between the master and his slave.[3] In fact, the

[1] *Summa Theologica,* IIa IIae, q. 104, art. 5.

[2] *Summa Theologica,* IIa IIae, q. 57, art. 4. St. Thomas' reference to Aristotle: *Omnia Opera, Graece et Latine* (2 vols., Parisiis: Editoribus Firmin-Didot et Sociis, 1883), Vol. II, *Ethica Nichomachea,* Lib. V, cap. VI, n. 8, p. 60.

[3] Cf. *Glossa ordinaria* ad c. 16, C. XVIII, q. 2, s.v. *quae acquisierit;* Abbas Panormitanus (Nicholaus de Tudeschis), *Commentaria in Quinque Libros Decretalium* (5 vols., in 7, Venetiis, 1588), ad c.23, X, *de voto et voti redemptione,* III, 24, n. 6; Guido de Bayso (or Baysio, or Baisio), *In Decretorum Volumen Commentaria (Rosarium),* ad c. 58, C. II, q. 7, n. 4.

religious subject in many instances was simply called a slave.[4] The authority of the master was called dominative, and the same term was used in description of the authority of the religious superior. Later, dominative power was used in description of the authority possessed by the head of any imperfect society.[5]

In order to set forth the true nature of the dominative power which, according to canon 501, § 1, is possessed by religious superiors, it is necessary to investigate the foundation or basis of this power. Various theories have been proposed by canonists in regard to this question. These theories may be reduced to three. The first theory proposes that the basis of the superior's dominative power lies in the vow of obedience which subjects profess on entering the religious state.[6] The second theory places the foundation of dominative power in the act of self-surrender implied by the subject's religious profession.[7] The third theory maintains that dominative power is possessed by the religious superior precisely because the community over which he rules is an imperfect society lawfully established by the Church. The fact that the community is a lawfully established society is the

---

[4] Cf. *Glossa ordinaria* ad c. 11, C. XII, q. 1, s.v. *possidere;* c. 2, C. XVII, q. 2; Guido de Bayso, *Rosarium,* ad c. 23, D. 54, s.v. *servitutem.*

[5] Blat, "De Potestate Superiorum in Religionibus Secundum Codicem I.C.," *CpRM,* XVI (1935), 324.

[6] Gerardus Kindt, *De Potestate Dominativa in Religione,* Universitas Catholica Louvaniensis Dissertationes, Series II, Tomus 34 (Brugis-Parisiis-Romae: Desclée de Brouwer, 1945), pp. 322-354; Biederlack-Führich, *De Religiosis,* pp. 54-55, n. 36; Coronata, *Institutiones,* I, 781, n. 603, nota 5; Gommarus Michiels, *Normae Generales Iuris Canonici, Commentarium Libri I Codicis Iuris Canonici* (2. ed., 2 vols., Tornaci: Desclée et Socii, 1949), I, 164 (hereinafter cited as *Normae Generales*); Sipos, *Enchiridion Iuris Canonici,* p. 325.

[7] Suarez, *Opera Omnia,* Tom. XIV-XVI, Tr. VI-VII; J. B. Raus, *De Sacrae Obedientiae Virtute et Voto* (Lugduni: Vitte, 1923), pp. 64-76; Beste, *Introductio in Codicem,* p. 331; Alphonsus Van Hove, *Commentarium Lovaniense in Codicem Iuris Canonici,* 1 vol. in 5 tomes, Tom. II, *De legibus ecclesiasticis* (Mechliniae-Romae: H. Dessain, 1930), 363-364, n. 357 (hereinafter cited as *De legibus ecclesiasticis*); Vermeersch-Creusen, *Epitome,* 458, n. 619; Hector Papi, *The Government of Religious Communities* (New York: P. J. Kenedy & Sons, 1919), p. 61; John Abbo-Jerome Hannan, *The Sacred Canons* (2 vols., St. Louis: B. Herder Book Co., 1952), I, 510.

basis and foundation of the dominative power possessed by the head of that community.[8]

In the view of the present writer, the last mentioned theory seems to have the most merit. The first two solutions seem to labor under serious defects, and appear less acceptable than the one espoused here.

In the preceding chapter it was shown that there must be present in every society an authority whereby the members are guided and directed to the end of the society. Authority necessarily inheres in the very nature of a society.[9] Furthermore, it was shown that the authority in the society resides in the head of the society and in those who have been selected to direct and guide its essential and integral parts. This authority is called dominative power.[10] It is enjoyed by the head of the non-exempt Congregation, since he is the head of an imperfect society which has been lawfully established by the Church.[11] The Superior, as the head of an imperfect society, enjoys this power over his subjects from the nature of the Congregation itself. It follows, then, that the theory which places the foundation of the superior's dominative power in the character of the Congregation as an imperfect society is worthy of acceptance. It is the nature of the society itself which gives rise to the authority in its superiors. It is by reason of the fact that the religious Institute is an im-

---

8 Larraona, "De Potestate Dominativa Publica," *ACII*, IV, 145-180; Adrien Cance, *Le Codc de Droit Canonique* (7. ed., 3 vols., Paris: J. Gabalda, 1946), II, 27, nota 3; W. A. Stanton, *De Societatibus sive Vivorum sive Mulierum in Communi Viventium sine Votis* (2. ed., Halifaxiae: Apud Custodiam Librariam Maioris Seminarii a Sanctissimo Corde B.V.M., 1936), pp. 111-114 (hereinafter cited as *De Societatibus*); Goyeneche, *Iuris Canonici Summa Principia de Religiosis* (Romae: Tip. Pol. "Cuore di Maria," 1938), p. 33, nota (15); Josephus Creusen, *Religieux et Religieuses d'après le Droit Ecclésiastique* (6. ed., Paris: Desclée de Brouwer, 1950), p. 35, n. 46; Lewis, *Chapters in Religious Institutes*, p. 52; H. Rothoff, *Le Droit des Sociétés sans Voeux* (Bruges: Desclée de Brouwer, 1949), pp. 116-119; Lucius Rodrigo, *Praelectiones Theologico-Morales Comillenses*, Vol. II, *De Legibus* (Santander: "Sal Terrae", 1944), 69, n. 93.

9 Cf. *supra*, pp. 29-30.

10 Cf. *supra*, p. 31.

11 Cf. *supra*, p. 34.

perfect society established by the Church, by reason of the fact that it has a definite end towards which all are to strive, that its superiors possess dominative power to rule their subjects.

Since it is the Church which institutes, approves and moderates religious Institutes,[12] it follows that the authority possessed by the superiors comes from the Church.[13] This can be shown from the fact that authority is a necessary adjunct of every society. Since it belongs exclusively to the Church to constitute the society known as the non-exempt religious Congregation, the Church in the very act of constituting and approving such a society confers on the superiors the dominative power for ruling which is essential for any imperfect society. In other words, the authority in the Congregation has the same origin as the Congregation itself.[14]

In proposing arguments in support of their theory, namely that the basis of dominative power is to be found in the vow of obedience made by the subjects, the proponents of this theory emphasize the fact that medieval canonists pointed to the vow of obedience as the basis for the subjection of religious to the superior.[15] They point also to the Code of Canon Law as sup-

---

[12] Can. 488, 1°, 3°.

[13] Rothoff, *Le Droit des Sociétés sans Voeux,* p. 117; Stanton, *De Societatibus,* p. 112.

[14] Cf. Ottaviani, *Institutiones,* I. 66, n. 26.

[15] Cf. Kindt, *De Potestate Dominativa,* pp. 57-64. This author (*op. cit.*, pp. 90-92) cites several texts from St. Thomas to show that St. Thomas clearly indicated that the vow of obedience is the foundation of the religious superior's dominative power. However, when these texts are examined, it seems, at least to the present writer, that St. Thomas in these texts clearly showed that the basis of the subjection of the subject to his religious superior is the vow of obedience. In these texts St. Thomas did not deal with the foundation of the dominative power as possessed by the superior. The texts cited by Kindt are the following: St. Thomas, *Quaestiones quodlibetales,* Quodl, I, qu. IX, art. 20; *Ibidem,* Quodl. III, qu. VI, art. 16. ad obiectionem; *Ibidem,* Quodl. X, qu. V, art. 10, ad 1^{m} et ad 3^{m}; *Opuscula,* Opusculum XVII, *De perfectione vitae spiritualis,* cap. X; *Quaestiones quodlibetales,* Quodl. III, qu. VI, art. 17, ad 6^{m}; *Ibidem,* Quodl. VI, qu. VI, art. 11; *In IV Sententiarum,* lib. IV, dist. 38, art. 4, quaestiuncula IV, sol. I, ad 5^{m}.

porting the same view.[16] However, it is one thing to show that the religious superior must be obeyed by a subject who has taken a vow of obedience. It is quite another thing to establish the basis of the superior's power to issue a command. It is granted that, if the subjects must obey, the superior must have the power to command. But it does not follow that the basis of the superior's power is the same as the basis of the subject's subjection.

If we seek the foundation of the superior's dominative power, we cannot look to the vow of obedience. The subjects do not confer authority on their religious superior. If they did, it would seem that they could take it away, and no one would admit that. Even the proponents of the theory which claims that dominative power is based on the vow grant that the vow of obedience is not the efficient cause of the superior's power.[17] However, it is asserted that the vow is the *causa exigitiva* of dominative power, that is, the vow demands or calls for the existence of dominative power in the superior[18]. But what need is there for the vow to call for the existence of a power which, as all admit, is inherent in the very nature of the non-exempt Congregation? The religious Institute is a lawfully established society. Therefore, the superior must have authority. There is no need for the vow of the subject to call for or demand a power which already exists prior to and independently of the vow.

Another argument opposed to the view that the vow of obedience is the basis or foundation of dominative power can be drawn from a consideration of those Institutes of men and women who live in community without vows. The superiors of such Institutes possess dominative power over their subjects according to canons 674 and 501, §1. [19] But since the subjects in such Institutes do not take vows, it cannot be maintained that the dominative power possessed by their superiors has its basis in the vow of obedience.

---

[16] Cf. Kindt, *op. cit.*, pp. 259-266.

[17] Kindt, *op. cit.*, p. 310.

[18] Kindt, *op. cit.*, pp. 310, 327-328.

[19] Schaefer, *De Religiosis*, p. 991; Beste, *Introductio in Codicem*, p. 460; Vermeersch-Creusen, *Epitome*, p. 629, n. 832.

The theory which places the basis of dominative power in the act of religious profession made by the subject also labors under difficulties. The foremost proponent of this theory, Franciscus Suarez, stated that the dominative power of the religious superior arises radically from the will of those who profess a religious rule and give themselves to a religious Institute with a promise and the obligation of obeying their superiors according to the rule they have professed.[20] If, then, dominative power arises from the will of the individual members of the Institute, it seems that a private person could give to his superior the right to issue commands which would be publicly recognized by the Church. Furthermore, the effect of the subject's donation would be greater than the cause. The subject cannot give to his superior that which he himself does not possess. The dominative power of the superior is greater and more extensive than the sum total of the individual and personal rights of his subjects.[21] Therefore the superior's dominative power cannot be said to arise from the will of his subjects.

It is better, then, in the view of the present writer, to maintain that the dominative power of superiors has its foundation in the fact that the non-exempt Congregation is a society which has been lawfully established by the Church. The vow of obedience and the act of profession are means whereby an individual becomes subject to the superior's dominative power, but the vow, or profession, is not to be confused with the basis or foundation of the dominative power which the superior possesses.

Authors have generally considered that the dominative power of religious superiors is a private power of ruling.[22] Ecclesiastical jurisdiction, on the other hand, has been defined as

---

[20] Suarez, *Opera Omnia, De Religione,* Tr. VII, lib. II c. 18, n. 5 — Vol. XVI, p. 218; Raus, *De Sacrae Obedientiae Virtute et Voto,* p. 65.

[21] Larraona, "De Potestate Dominativa Publica," *ACII,* IV, p. 162, n. 17.

[22] Kindt, *De Potestate Dominativa,* p. 322; Raus, *De Sacrae Obedientiae Virtute et Voto,* p. 65; Beste, *Introductio in Codicem,* p. 215; Josephus Pejska, *Jus Canonicum Religiosorum* (3. ed., Friburgi Brisgoviae: Herder, 1927), p. 229.

a public power. It is proper to certain superiors and derives from Christ, or from the Church through a canonical mission. It authorizes the one possessing it to rule the baptized in relation to their eternal salvation.[23] While none would maintain that dominative power is identified with ecclesiastical jurisdiction, Larraona gives sound reasons for maintaining that dominative power is not a purely private power of ruling. He demonstrates that the dominative power possessed by a religious superior differs from the dominative power possessed by the head of an amicable society whose members freely unite to attain some worthwhile end, be it philanthropic, literary, or scientific. The heads of such societies possess dominative power, but it is of a purely private character.[24] Even in societies which have a juridic character, such as a pious union or a confraternity, the superiors possess dominative power which is strictly private in character. Such dominative power differs profoundly from the dominative power possessed by the superiors of religious Congregations. Larraona, therefore, proposes that dominative power be divided into two classes: *private* and *public* dominative power.[25]

He defends the public character of dominative power of religious superiors by showing that religious superiors perform many acts of a public character, and these acts are recognized as such by the Church.[26] It is the religious superior who in the name of the Church receives the public vows of those who are admitted into a public state in the Church.[27] The religious superior can dismiss his subjects from the religious state, and even reduce them to the lay state, if they be in minor Orders when they are dismissed by him.[28] He can prevent one of his clerical

---

[23] Ottaviani, *Institutiones,* I, 202.

[24] "De Potestate Dominativa Publica," *ACII,* IV, 168; cf. *supra,* p. 30.

[25] "De Potestate Dominativa Publica," *ACII,* IV, 148; Cf. also Clancy, *The Local Religious Superior,* p. 9; J. Delchard, "Elements of Canon Law," *Religious Sisters,* being the English version of *Directoire des Supérieures* and *Les Adaptations de la Vie Religieuse* (Westminster, Maryland: The Newman Press, 1951), p. 172.

[26] Larraona, "De Potestate Dominativa Publica," *ACII,* IV, 165 ff.

[27] Cans. 543; 572, § 1, 2°, 6°; 1308, § 1.

[28] Cans. 571, § 1; 637; 647; 648.

subjects from advancing to sacred Orders.[29] The local superior is authorized by the Code to exercise many public functions which ordinarily belong to a pastor. Thus the superior has the right to administer Viaticum and Extreme Unction to the religious, novices, and to other persons dwelling day and night in the religious house.[30] Funeral rights, which normally are proper to the pastor, are granted to religious superiors in reference to their professed subjects and novices.[31] In clerical religious Institutes the permission to establish a new house carries with it the right to have a church or a public oratory in connection with the religious house.[32] The religious rector of such a church or oratory has parochial rights with reference to his religious subjects.[33] From these examples it can be seen that in the exercise of his dominative power the religious superior performs actions which certainly are public in character and which are recognized as public by the Church.

It is evident, then, that the dominative power of a religious superior is certainly not of the same private character as the dominative power exercised by the head of a purely amicable society. It seems to the present writer that Larraona's use of the term *public dominative power,* when describing the authority of a religious superior, is fully justified. Such a term does not infringe upon or derogate from the notion of the power of jurisdiction. Rather, it serves to clarify the concept of the dominative power of religious superiors and clearly differentiates it from purely *private dominative power.*[34]

On March 26, 1952, the Pontifical Commission for the Interpretation of the Code replied to a question concerning the dominative power of superiors. It was asked whether the pre-

---

[29] Can. 970.

[30] Can. 514, § 1.

[31] Can. 1221, § 1.

[32] Can. 497, § 2.

[33] Cf. Larraona, "De Potestate Paroeciali relate ad Religiosos," *CpR,* VIII (1927), 37-38.

[34] Cf. Clancy, *The Local Religious Superior,* p. 9.

scriptions of canons 197, 199, 206-209, which deal with the power of jurisdiction, are to be applied to dominative power unless the nature of the matter or the text or the context of the law prohibits such application. An affirmative answer was given.[35] In virtue of this authentic declaration it is now possible to substitute the words "dominative power" for the words "power of jurisdiction" in the canons mentioned in the reply. Thus, canon 197, § 1: "Ordinary dominative power is that which the law itself attaches to an office. Delegated dominative power is that which is not attached to an office, but is committed to a person." Similarly, canon 199, § 1, reads as follows when the substitution is made: "One who enjoys ordinary dominative power can delegate it to another wholly or in part, unless the law expressly rules otherwise." A corresponding substitution may be made in the other canons mentioned in the reply.

This authentic declaration indirectly confirms, though not in express words, the opinion that the dominative power mentioned in canon 501, § 1, is a public power. If it is not a public power, how then could the rules and principles governing jurisdiction be applied to it? [36]

Before it be undertaken to discuss the extent of the dominative power of the religious superior it may be useful to offer a definition of that power. The dominative power which, according to canon 501, § 1, is possessed by religious superiors is a public power of governing, although distinct from jurisdiction. It is limited by the prescriptions of the Constitutions of the religious Institute and the general law of the Church, and arises from the very nature of the imperfect society. It is granted by the Church to religious superiors as a means whereby they can govern and direct the actions of their subjects to the attainment of the end of the religious Institute.

---

[35] *AAS,* XLIV (1952), 497.

[36] Cf. J. B. Fuertes, "De Potestate Dominativa in Religionibus Non Exemptis," *CpRM,* XXXII (1953), 344.

Article 2. The Extent of the Dominative Power of the Local Superior

Besides stating that the local superior in non-exempt Congregations possesses dominative power, the Code enumerates many rights and obligations of the superior for the direction and guidance of his subjects. These rights and obligations receive mention not only in those sections of the Code that deal specifically with religious, but also in other sections of the Code.

In attempting to depict the dominative power of the local superior as delineated in the Code, one must examine at least some of the superior's functions in order to determine their relationship with dominative power. It is the opinion of the present writer that all the rights and obligations attributed by the Code to the local superior in a non-exempt Congregation are expressions of his dominative power. Larraona is the foremost exponent of this view.[37] It is of importance to note that we seek to set forth not merely the nature of dominative power as it is in itself, but precisely the nature of that dominative power which canon 501, § 1, states to be characteristic of the religious superior.

The dominative power of the religious superior may be examined in two different aspects or phases, namely, the social aspect and the personal or individual aspect.[38] These are not separate and distinct from dominative power, but are rather two phases of the same power, both of which are necessary for the religious superior to exercise the control and direction which the Church expects of a religious superior. All the rights and obligations attributed by the Code to the non-exempt local superior can be reduced to either the social or personal aspect of his dominative power. In other words, when the local superior exercises the faculties granted to him by the Code, he is exercising the dominative power mentioned in canon 501, § 1.

---

[37] Larraona, "De Potestate Dominativa Publica," *ACII*, IV, p. 178, n. 30; cf. Coronata, *Institutiones*, I, 641, n. 527; Pejska, *Jus Canonicum Religiosorum*, p. 230.

[38] Larraona, *ibid.*, p. 165, n. 18, b); pp. 169-177, nn. 20-26.

The superior exercises the social aspect of his dominative power when he rules his community in so far as it is considered as a particular social entity. The subjects of the superior are ruled not as individuals but inasmuch as they are members of that social entity. Many of the faculties granted by the Code either directly to the local superior or to the superior designated by the Constitutions of the Institute are granted so that the superior can exercise a general social control over his community. Thus, the administration of the temporal goods of the house is committed to the local superior.[39] However, the Code prescribes that each religious house shall have its own procurator, who is to exercise his office under the direction of the local superior.[40] The general spiritual formation of his subjects as religious[41] and the supervision of their clerical studies[42] are committed to the care of the superior. The superior can, in virtue of the social aspect of his dominative power, issue to his subjects precepts through which he urges them to adhere to the Constitutions and rules of the Institute.[43] The superior designated

---

[39] Can. 532.

[40] Can. 516, § 3.

[41] Cans. 553 ff.

[42] Cans 587-591.

[43] Canonists unanimously agree that the superior who possesses dominative power can issue a precept to one of his subjects. Whether or not such individual dominative precepts are dealt with in canon 24 is disputed. Van Hove (*De legibus ecclesiasticis,* p. 362, n. 356) is the leading exponent of the view that canon 24 refers only to the precepts issued by those who possess jurisdiction. His arguments are effectively counteracted by the arguments of Michiels (*Normae Generales,* I, 693). In the view of the present writer, the opinion of Michiels is the more solidly founded. According to this view, canon 24 also applies, at least by analogy, to dominative precepts.

Canon 24, it is true, in the words of the text, does not specifically mention dominative precepts, but it is also true that the text does not state that the precepts dealt with are only such as are issued by one who possesses jurisdiction. The words used by the lawgiver are most general, "*praecepta singulis data,*" and can be applied equally to both types of precepts. The fact that dominative precepts cannot be juridically enforced does not mean, as Van Hove asserted, that they are therefore to be excluded from the ambit of canon 24. This canon demands the prescribed solemnities in the issuing of precepts in order that they may be enforced jurid-

by the Constitutions, and thus not necessarily the major superior,[44] can dismiss novices,[45] receive the religious profession of his subjects,[46] and can exclude from the renewal of the vows a subject whose temporary vows have expired.[47] The Code further grants to local superiors the faculty to dismiss perpetually professed subjects in urgent cases, with the consent of his council and the local ordinary.[48]

These and other rights granted by the Code to the local superior look to the good of the whole society. They are social in character and are an expression of one phase of his general power of government which is called dominative power.

Besides the social aspect of the dominative power possessed by the local religious superior, another phase of his dominative power remains to be considered, namely, the personal or individual phase. When the superior's dominative power is exercised under this personal aspect, it has for its immediate object the direction and control of his subjects as individuals. The superior in exercising his dominative power in their regard seeks to guide and direct them in the pursuit of the perfection which they sought to attain by becoming affiliated with the religious Institute.

In order to enable the local superior to exert the necessary control over his subjects, the Code grants him a number of facul-

ically, *and also* in order to ensure their continued binding force after the loss of office of the one issuing the precepts. This latter provision can certainly be verified in the case of dominative precepts. In other words, the obligation of dominative precepts will cease with the loss of office of the one issuing them, unless they had been issued according to the solemnities prescribed in canon 24. Whether or not a local superior can issue a common precept to the whole community, considered as a unit, is another disputed question. There is no explicit mention in the Code of such common precepts. If the superior issues a precept to the whole community, it is to be considered as having been given to each individual member. (Cf. Michiels, *Normae Generales,* I, 694-698).

[44] Cf. Schaefer, *De Religiosis,* p. 205, n. 1522.

[45] Can. 571, § 1.

[46] Can. 572, § 1, 6°.

[47] Can. 637.

[48] Can. 653.

ties which can be reduced to the personal phase of his dominative power. When he employs these faculties the superior is exercising a phase of the dominative power mentioned in canon 501, § 1.

By way of example the following instances may be cited. The Code grants to religious superiors the right and the duty in case of sickness to administer, personally or through a delegate, both Holy Viaticum and Extreme Unction to the professed, to the novices, and also to other persons who dwell day and night in the religious house by reason of employment, education, hospitality or health.[49] The superior's rights with reference to the funeral services of the professed religious, the novices, and the household guests and employees are clearly set forth by the Code.[50] The faithful and regular performance of the exercises of piety so necessary for advancement in personal sanctification is committed to the care of the local superior.[51] The superior is to see that each of his subjects makes a retreat each year; assists at Holy Mass daily unless he be legitimately impeded; makes a daily meditation; performs the other exercises of piety prescribed by the Rules and Constitutions; and goes to confession at least once a week. The local religious superior must also see to it that clerics who are subject to him make a daily visit to the Blessed Sacrament; recite the rosary; and examine their conscience each day.[52]

From the above mentioned examples it can be seen that the Code grants to a local superior the authority necessary to direct the personal sanctification of his subjects. This is but another phase of the dominative power mentioned in canon 501, § 1. It is not a power distinct from dominative power, but is, like the social aspect of dominative power, merely another phase of that general authority whereby he rules and directs his subjects. In other words, it is a manifestation of the authority conceded to him by canon 501, § 1.

---

[49] Can. 514, § 1.

[50] Can. 1221, §§ 1, 2.

[51] Can. 595, § 1.

[52] Can. 125, 2°; cf. Schaefer, *De Religiosis,* p. 635, n. 1064.

The expressed view, namely that the various rights granted by the Code to the non-exempt superior can be considered an expression of his dominative power, is not universally accepted by contemporary canonists.

Gerard Kindt maintains that, apart from and distinct from his dominative power, the superior possesses other powers.[53] He would reduce some of the faculties granted by the Code to what he calls the partial exemption enjoyed by non-exempt Congregations.[54] There are other faculties which, so he states, cannot be reduced to dominative power but must be considered as pertaining to a distinct power which he calls the *potestas superioritatis.* He considers this *potestas superioritatis* as being synonymous with social, economic, domestic or administrative power.[55]

However, a study of this view shows that it contains certain defects and that moreover it does not in fact impair the value of the explanation of the general nature and extent of the dominative power of the local superior.

Kindt states that not all the rights of government granted to the religious superior can be classified under the notion of dominative power, for some of these rights were formerly possessed by the pastor or by the local ordinary. The example of the right of the religious superior to administer Viaticum to his subjects is cited.[56] This is a right which ordinarily would have been possessed by the pastor for the faithful of his territory.[57] When this right of the pastor is transferred to the religious superior, so Kindt asserts, then its exercise cannot be considered an exercise of the superior's dominative power. The local superior can exercise this parochial right because, in addition to his dominative power, he enjoys what is called partial exemption.[58]

---

[53] *De Potestate Dominativa,* pp. 266-286.
[54] *Op. cit.,* pp. 275-278.
[55] *Op. cit.,* pp. 341-345.
[56] *Op. cit.,* p. 276.
[57] Can. 850.
[58] *Op. cit.,* p. 276.

Another example is cited in support of this same view. The religious superior exercises certain rights in caring for the formation of his clerical subjects. The superior enjoys these rights because his Institute enjoys partial exemption. Such rights cannot be considered as an expression of dominative power. The power which the bishop exercises in the formation of his clerical subjects is not a dominative power. Why, then, it is asked, should it be called a dominative power when it is exercised by the religious superior? [59]

By way of reply it can well be granted that the Code has conferred on the local religious superior certain rights which ordinarily would have been exercised by the pastor or the bishop. However, if we examine the rights of the pastor which are now exercised by the religious superior, it is of importance to determine whether these rights involve the use of jurisdiction. If the pastor in exercising the rights now conferred on local religious superiors exercises only dominative power, it seems that the objection falls. If it is a use of dominative power when exercised by the pastor, it seems that there can be no objection to reducing that same right to the dominative power of the superior.

The question to be answered then is: Does the pastor enjoy jurisdiction? The Code states that the pastor has ordinary jurisdiction to hear the confessions of those who are in his territory and also the confessions of his subjects anywhere.[60] However, authors agree that the pastor's jurisdiction is limited to the internal forum of conscience.[61] He does not have ordinary jurisdiction in the external forum (except for the cases expressly stated in the Code, namely, in cans. 1044, 1045, 1245). No parochial function requires this type of jurisdiction.[62] The pastor is able to carry out his duties in reference to the care of souls

---

[59] Kindt, *op. cit.*, p. 277.

[60] Can. 873, § 1.

[61] Coronata, *Institutiones,* I, p. 580, n. 480, f); Beste, *Introductio in Codicem,* p. 289; Abbo-Hannan, *The Sacred Canons,* I, 446; J. Brys, *Juris Canonici Compendium* (10. ed., 2. ed. post codicem, 2 vols., Brugis: Desclée Desclée de Brouwer et Sii, 1947-1949), I, p. 442, n. 543.

[62] Vermeersch-Creusen, *Epitome,* I, p. 406, n. 546.

with that type of power which is called dominative,[63] domestic or economic.[64] This was the common opinion even before the Code, as Pope Benedict XIV testified.[65]

Thus, since the exercise of parochial functions does not necessarily involve the use of ordinary jurisdiction, it follows, then, that when some of these parochial functions are committed to the religious superior, the faculties to exercise these functions can be considered an expression of the superior's dominative power.

Even though it is granted that the bishop in caring for the spiritual and intellectual formation of his seminarians may, on occasion, invoke his power of jurisdiction, the religious superior, in caring for the training of his clerical subjects exercises only dominative power. There is no need to reduce the faculties granted by the Code in this regard to a partial exemption enjoyed by non-exempt Congregations. There are some rights, it is true, which are so conditioned upon the power of jurisdiction that they cannot be exercised by means of an inferior type of power, e.g., the faculty of forgiving sins, the faculty to make laws, the faculty to impose canonical penalties. These faculties are so conditioned upon the power of jurisdiction that they cannot be exercised by one who possesses only dominative power. However, there are other faculties which for their use are not strictly conditioned upon the possession of jurisdiction, and accordingly can be exercised by one who enjoys but a dominative power.[66]

A superior who possesses both jurisdiction and dominative power can command one of his subjects by reason of his power of jurisdiction. He can oblige another subject to carry out the same command by invoking his dominative power. Thus, there is no evident contradiction if it is maintained that the bishop com-

---

63 Cance, *Le Code de Droit Canonique,* I, 415.

64 Vermeersch-Creusen, *Epitome,* I, p. 406, n. 546.

65 *De Synodo Dioecesana* (3 vols., Romae: Ex Typographia Jo. Baptistae Cannetti, 1783), Lib. V, cap. IV.

66 Larraona, "De Potestate Dominativa Publica," *ACII,* IV, pp. 167-168, n. 19.

mands his seminarians by his power of jurisdiction. The religious superior, however, in giving commands in similar matters exercises only his dominative power. It may also be added that it is not clearly established that the bishop's supervision over his seminarians is an act of jurisdiction. In fact, the contrary seems more likely.

The Code clearly states that dominative power is possessed by a non-exempt superior. To maintain that the local superior's exercise of some of the faculties granted by the Code involves the use of jurisdiction seems to run counter to the provisions of the Code. The Code does not grant him ordinary jurisdiction. The conclusion, then, is that in the cited examples there is no valid reason why such faculties cannot be considered an expression of the dominative power of the superior.

Since the Code states that religious superiors have dominative power over their subjects, Kindt maintains that when the local superior exercises control over the novices and postulants he is not exercising his dominative power.[67] Similarly, the administration of temporal goods involves the use of a power different from dominative power.[68] The reason for this assertion is based on a restrictive interpretation as deriving from the phrase "over their subjects" in canon 501, § 1. Novices and the administration of goods are considered to be outside the ambit of dominative power, for the reason that novices are not subjects of the superior, and the administration of temporal goods is a faculty not exercised directly over subjects.[69] According to this view, novices are governed and temporal goods are administered by what is called the *potestas superioritatis.* Such a new term, in the view of the supporters of this theory, seems to be equivalent to social, economic or domestic power.

Kindt contends that novices are not governed by means of the local superior's dominative power. Only by religious profession, so he contends, does one become a subject of the su-

---

[67] *De Potestate Dominativa,* p. 341.

[68] Kindt, *op. cit.,* p. 342.

[69] Kindt, *op. cit.,* p. 260.

perior's dominative power. This view cannot be accepted. By the very fact that novices have of their own free will entered the novitiate they have associated themselves with a social group. They must, by that fact, submit to the authority possessed by the head of the group. They do in fact become subject to the local superior and are bound to obey him.[70] The superior, as head of the society which the novices have freely joined, has authority to rule those who make up that society. The Code calls the authority possessed by the local superior dominative power. The novices are subject to this dominative power.[71] The extent of the superior's dominative power in reference to novices is not as great as it is in reference to professed religious. Nevertheless, the novices are subject to the dominative power of the local superior in all that pertains to the general government of the house.[72]

In a similar manner, though in a lesser degree, household guests are also subject to the dominative power of the local superior.[73] They too have freely associated themselves with a society and for this reason are subject to the dominative power possessed by the head of that society. The local superior will be able to exercise his dominative power in their regard in order to maintain the good order of the house. As long as they remain associated with the religious house they are subject to the authority of the superior, although they are free to leave whenever they so desire.

---

70 Can. 561, § 2.

71 Pejska, *Ius Canonicum Religiosorum*, p. 139; Albertus Blat, *Commentarium Textus Codicis Iuris Canonici* (5 vols. in 6, Lib. II, *Ius de Religiosis*, 3. ed., Romae: "Apud Angelicum," 1938), II, 344 (hereinafter cited as *Ius de Religiosis*); Larraona, "Commentarium Codicis," *CpRM*, XXIV (1943), 28; Dominicus Prümmer, *Manuale Iuris Canonici* (5. ed., Friburgi-Brisgoviae: Herder, 1927), p. 249; Van Hove, *De legibus ecclesiasticis*, p. 364, n. 357.

72 Clancy, *The Local Religious Superior*, p. 38.

73 Thomas Bowe, *Religious Superioresses*, The Catholic University of America Canon Law Studies, n. 228 (Washington, D.C.: The Catholic University of America Press, 1946), pp. 66-67, 78-79.

The power of the local superior over novices and household guests need not be reduced to a new entity, namely the *potestas superioritatis,* a term not used by the Code. The dominative power that the local superior exercises over novices and guests is the same power, in a lesser degree, that he exercises over professed religious.

The superior's rights to administer the temporal goods of the community, Kindt states, are not manifestations of his dominative power since dominative power can be exercised only over his subjects. Inasmuch as the powers of administration do not directly refer to the subjects, they are to be classified as proofs of another power of the superior, his economic power, or his *potestas superioritatis.*[74]

It is true that the administration of temporal goods may not have direct reference to the individual subject of the superior. However, the nature of the power possessed by the head of a society demands not only that it touch the personal actions of the individual members, but also that it concern itself with managing the temporalities possessed by the society as a whole.[75] In a religious Congregation the goods of the society are possessed in common. The society itself, being a moral person, cannot administer its own goods, but must act through the lawfully constituted head of the society. The superior in performing acts of temporal administration is exercising the general power of ruling the society, which canon 501, § 1, calls dominative power. His acts of administration certainly have reference to his subjects, for he is dealing with temporalities possessed by them as a moral unit. It seems, then, that there can be no objection to considering the superior's faculties over temporalities, as an expression of his dominative power.

---

[74] *De Potestate Dominativa,* p. 341.

[75] Pejska, *Ius Canonicum Religiosorum,* p. 341; Vermeersch-Creusen, *Epitome,* I, p. 459, n. 620; Blat, *Commentarium,* II, 120; Guidus Cocchi, *Commentarium in Codicem Iuris Canonici ad Usum Scholarum* (8 vols., Vol. IV (Lib. II, *De Personis,* Pars II, *De Religiosis*), 4. ed., Taurinorum Augustae: Ex Officina Libraria Marietti, 1946), IV, p. 42, n. 23, c) (Hereinafter cited as *Commentarium*).

Some authors maintain that in addition to, and also quite distinct from, his dominative power the superior can command his religious subjects by virtue of a power which arises from the vow which his religious subjects have taken. This power is referred to as *potestas ex voto*.[76]

However, it cannot be maintained that the superior possesses any new and distinct power by reason of the vow of his subjects, because they are already bound to carry out the legitimate commands of their superior by reason of his dominative power. He can, it is true, intensify the obligation of obeying his commands by reminding his subjects that they have taken a vow to God to obey the legitimate commands of their lawfully constituted superiors. But the superior does not, apart from his dominative power, acquire a new power by reason of the vow of his subject. He is merely able to fortify or render more binding the commands which he issues by reason of the dominative power he possesses.[77]

The extent of the dominative power possessed by the local superior is such that it embraces all the various faculties granted by the Code to local superiors. When he cares for the spiritual welfare of his subjects, directs their training as clerics, exerts control over the novices, or administers the temporal goods, he is exercising his dominative power.

The only name that the Code gives to the authority possessed by the local superior is dominative power. There is no mention of *domestic, social* or *economic power,* or of the *potestas superioritatis.* As Pejska noted, such a sub-division serves no practical purpose in the study of this subject and can only prove burdensome.[78] After stating that superiors do possess dominative power, the Code in various places indicates the extension of that power. The Church is free to augment or restrict that power. As the law stands today, all the faculties granted to the local

[76] Raus, *De Sacrae Obedientiae Virtute et Voto,* pp. 87-109.

[77] Van Hove, *De legibus ecclesiasticis,* p. 364, n. 357; Pejska, *Ius Canonicum Religiosorum,* pp. 139-140; Stanton, *De Societatibus,* p. 114.

[78] *Ius Canonicum Religiosorum,* p. 139.

superior by the Code are, in the opinion of the present writer, an expression of that one general power of ruling, namely dominative power. This is the broader view regarding the nature and the extent of dominative power, but one that seems justified by the Code and worthy of acceptance.

CHAPTER IV

The Candidate for the Office of Local Superior

Article 1. Qualities Required in the Candidate

The consideration of the qualifications for the office of local superior may be positive or negative. Not only must the subject possess certain qualifications which render him eligible for the position, but he must furthermore be free from anything which disqualifies him from receiving this office.

The local superior has the obligation to govern the society dependent on him in such a way that it may attain its twofold end. Every religious Institute is expected to fulfill its particular mission in the Church and to promote the sanctification of its members. Such considerations demand that the superior possess the qualities of humility, piety, firmness, studiousness in the observance of discipline, patience, charity, knowledge, prudence, affability, justice and good example.[1] The Code does not list any specific positive requirements for the candidate to this office, but leaves these matters to be determined in detail by the Constitutions of the individual Congregations. The specifications made by the Constitutions on these matters are of great importance, and they must be carefully considered and adhered to by the major superior who appoints the local superior, or by those who have the right to elect him.

In presenting the negative qualifications for the office of religious superior, canon 504 concerns itself directly with those matters alone which render a subject disqualified or ineligible for the office of major superior. It states that religious are not qualified for the position of major superior if they have not been professed at least ten years in the Institute. If they were born of unlawful wedlock they are also disqualified. When the office involved is that of Superior General of the Institute, those

[1] Cocchi, *Commentarium,* IV, p. 44, n. 24.

who have not completed the age of forty years are to be excluded. Those who have not completed the age of thirty years are barred from the office of other major superiors. Since this canon considers religious who are not qualified for the office of major superior, there is no reason why the disqualifying provisions of the canon should be applied to the candidate for the office of local superior. If the legislator had wished to do so, he could have stated that these provisions should also have reference to the office of local superior. He did not do so. It is left to the Constitutions of the individual Institute to determine the positive and negative qualifications required in the candidate.[2] Usually the Constitutions make specific provisions on these points.[3] If, however, the Constitutions make no mention, for example, of the requirement of age or of the fact of legitimacy in the candidate for local superior, canon 504 cannot be urged to prevent the appointment of a subject who has not completed his thirtieth year of age or whose birth does not derive through lawful wedlock.

In considering the negative qualifications for the office of local superior, one must of necessity give heed to those laws of the Code which disqualify anyone from any office. Canon 154 states that offices to which there is attached the care of souls cannot be validly conferred upon clerics who are not as yet ordained priests. This law applies to the office of the local superior, to whom the care of the souls of his subjects has been entrusted.[4] The religious who has been deprived of the right to be elected to office *(vox passiva)* cannot be promoted to the

---

[2] Ludovicus Fanfani, *De Iure Religiosorum* (3. ed., Rovigo: Istituto Padano di Arti Grafiche, 1949), p. 84, n. 48, B); Vermeersch-Creusen, *Epitome,* I, p. 462, n. 622; Abbo-Hannan, *The Sacred Canons,* I, 514.

[3] E.g., *The Constitutions and Rules of the Congregation of the Missionary Oblates of the Most Holy and Immaculate Virgin Mary* (Rome, 1945), Art. 582: "The Provincial chooses the local Superiors from among the more outstanding priests of the Institute, who have been in perpetual vows for three years."

[4] Schaefer, *De Religiosis,* p. 219, n. 469; Coronata, *Institutiones,* I, 653, n. 539, b).

office of local superior.[5] One who has by the commission of a crime been disqualified from holding all ecclesiastical offices, or specifically a religious office, is similarly disbarred.[6] The religious who has apostatized from the religious organization, even though he later returned to his Institute, is deprived forever of the active right of casting a vote and of the passive right of receiving a vote in an ecclesiastical election.[7] Religious who are under the censure of excommunication, who are under personal interdict, or who also are under suspension, are incapable of acquiring any office or position in the Church, provided that this penalty rests upon them after the use of a declaratory or a condemnatory sentence.[8] Similarly, a religious who has incurred infamy, whether of law or of fact, is disqualified from holding any ecclesiastical office.[9]

The above-mentioned delicts are punished with the vindicative penalty of incapacity for the holding of office. The purpose of this penalty is directed more to the restoration of the good order of society than to the punishment of the culprit.[10] The legislator also intends to safeguard the subjects of a superior by demanding that those who are guilty of such crimes be barred from such a position of trust.

Article 2. The Appointment of the Local Superior

The religious superior can be constituted in office in one of three ways: by way of appointment; by way of election;

---

[5] Fanfani, *De Iure Religiosorum*, p. 84, n. 48, C), 2°; Schaefer, *De Religiosis*, p. 219, n. 468; Philippus Maroto, *Institutiones Iuris Canonici* (2 vols., Romae: apud Commentarium pro Religiosis; Matriti: Editorial del Corazón de Maria, 1919), I, 695, n. 589, A), e). Maroto stated that a religious who has been deprived of eligibility for office is disqualified from holding office in his Institute. Thus, even though the local superior is appointed and not elected, the subject who has been deprived of the right of being elected for office must be considered as being unsuited (*non idoneus*) and hence ineligible (cf. can. 153) for the office of local superior. Cf. cans. 2331, § 2; 2336, § 1; 2360; 2368, § 1; 2389.

[6] E.g., cans. 2345; 2346; 2390, § 2; 2394; 2395; 2313, §§ 1, 2.

[7] Can. 2385.

[8] Cans. 2265; 2275, 3°; 2283.

[9] Can. 2294.

[10] Cf. can. 2286.

and by way of postulation.[11] The Code does not indicate which method is to be used in the selection of the local superior. Since the Code is silent on this point, it is left to the Constitutions of the various Congregations to determine this matter. However, it is a common practice in non-exempt Congregations for the major superior to appoint the local superior.[12] The Constitutions of the Institute determine whether the appointment shall be made by the major superior as acting in his own personal right, or as acting only in view of the previously furnished advice or consent of his council.[13]

In the event that the local superior receives his designation for office by way of an ecclesiastical election, a few points on election and postulation may be noted. The rules governing ecclesiastical elections are stated in canons 160-182. These rules govern the election of the local superior unless approved particular law provides otherwise.[14] The electors must abstain from seeking votes directly or indirectly for themselves or for others.[15] In fact, canon 506, § 1, demands that in Institutes of men religious, the members of the chapter shall, before they proceed to the election of major superiors, promise under oath to elect those who, as they deem before God, should be elected. This is not demanded, however, by the common law in the election of the local superior.[16] If, however, the Constitutions demand such an oath before all elections, such a provision would obviously have to be complied with before the election of a local superior.[17]

Postulation may be defined as the voted decision of an electoral college to petition a competent superior for the appointment to a vacant office, by way of dispensation, of a definite person who is ineligible for election because of some canonical

11 Cf. can. 148, § 1; Fanfani, *De Iure Religiosorum*, p. 139; Schaefer, *De Religiosis*, p. 229, n. 482; De Carlo, *Jus Religiosorum*, p. 99, n. 115.

12 Balmes, *Les Religieux à voeux simples*, p. 60.

13 Schaefer, *De Religiosis*, p. 229, n. 482.

14 Can. 507, § 1.

15 Can. 507, § 2.

16 Larraona, "Commentarium Codicis," *CpR*, VII (1926), p. 446, n. 34, a), I; De Carlo, *Jus Religiosorum*, p. 110, n. 132.

17 De Carlo, *Jus Religiosorum*, p. 110, n. 132.

defect or impediment.[18] Postulation as a means for selecting a religious superior should be permitted only in an extraordinary case provided the Constitutions do not prohibit it.[19] If the Constitutions make no mention of postulation, it can be invoked in extraordinary cases, since the silence of the Constitutions is not equivalent to a prohibition.[20]

As indicated above, the local superior in a non-exempt Congregation is generally appointed to this office. The Supreme Pontiff may appoint any religious superior.[21] The right of the Roman Pontiff to confer any office in the Church derives from his primacy, and this prerogative is his under the divine law itself.[22] However, it would be exceptional for the Pontiff to exercise his right in the appointment of a local superior. Normally the Constitutions designate the major superior who is competent to make the appointment, and they specify whether the appointing superior is to act in his own personal right, or only in view of the previously furnished consent or advice of his council. In making the appointment to the office of local superior, the major superior is bound by the provisions of the common law and by the Constitutions of his own Institute. As indicated in Article 1 of this chapter,[23] the subject to be appointed must be free from any impediment which would disqualify him from office by reason of the common law itself or also the particular law of the Institute.

Article 3. The Term of Office of the Local Superior

Minor local superiors are not permitted to hold office for more than three years; when this term has elapsed, they may be reappointed to the same office for a second term if the Constitutions permit it, but not immediately for a third term in the

---

18 Cf. 179, § 1; Abbo-Hannan, *The Sacred Canons,* I, p. 239, n. 179.

19 Can. 507, § 3.

20 Beste, *Introductio ad Codicem,* p. 338; Abbo-Hannan, *The Sacred Canons,* I, pp. 517, 518, n. 507, 3.

21 Cf. can. 1431; Schaefer, *De Religiosis,* p. 229, n. 483.

22 Abbo-Hannan, *The Sacred Canons,* II, 664.

23 Cf. *supra,* pp. 61-62.

same religious house.[24] Each of these provisions of canon 505 will now be considered.

A local superior is bound by the provisions of canon 505 regarding his temporary tenure of office. The ones in charge of filial houses, however, are not superiors properly so called, and hence are not subject to the provisions of the canon under consideration.[25] The difficulties that might be encountered in consequence of the relatively short tenure of office of the superior of a school or hospital can oftentimes be obviated through the fact that he will be allowed to remain in charge of the school or hospital even after the appointment of a new superior with authority as regards the religious discipline.[26]

When the Code declares that the office of local superior may not be held for more than three years it does not mean that a superior could not be appointed for a period of time less than three years.[27] If the Constitutions provide for the appointment of a local superior who is to hold office at the will *(ad nutum)* of the major superior, such a local superior should be confirmed in office at the end of his three years in office, and he is not, without an Apostolic indult, to be maintained in office for more than six continuous years in the same house.[28]

The period of three years is to be measured according to the rule indicated in canon 34. Thus the years in the superior's term of office are to be taken as they are in the calendar, and if the time of the appointment does not coincide with the beginning of the day, the first day is not counted, and the term of three years expires when the final day which bears the same date is completed.[29]

---

[24] Can. 505.

[25] *PCI*, 2-3 iun. 1918 — *AAS*, X (1918), 344.

[26] Cf. Schaefer, *De Religiosis*, p. 223, n. 473.

[27] Coronata, *Institutiones*, I, 656; Schaefer, *De Religiosis*, p. 222; Larraona, "Commentarium Codicis," *CpR*, VII (1926), 378, c), I.

[28] Schaefer, *De Religiosis*, p. 222; Larraona, "Commentarium Codicis," *CpR*, VII (1926), 378, c), II.

[29] Can. 34, § 3, 3°.

In the absence of specification in the letters of appointment the Constitutions and the legitimate customs of the Institute should be consulted for a determining of the precise beginning of the three-year term of office. Thus, for example, the Constitutions may determine that, even though the subject has been legitimately appointed by his major superior, he cannot begin to function as superior until he has formally taken possession of his office in some prescribed way. Such provisions would of course have binding force.[30] The common law, however, does not require the actual taking of possession of the office, and the term will usually begin on the day on which the letters of appointment are signed.[31] This will be so even though the superior, when appointed, was at a great distance from the house to which he has been assigned. The beginning of a juridic reckoning of time depends not on some accidental fact, but rather on some legitimate act,[32] which in this case is the written and signed appointment to the office.[33] Canon 38 states that rescripts by which a favor is granted without the ministry of an executor take effect from the moment at which the letters were issued.

If the office of local superior has been obtained as the result of an election or a postulation, the three-year term will commence on the day on which the election is confirmed or the postulation accepted.[34]

Since canon 505 states that the local superior should hold office for three or at most six years, it follows that, when the superior's term of office has elapsed, he automatically loses his authority. However, by the provisions of the Constitutions, or by legitimate custom, or by the action of the major superior, a prorogation could be granted.[35] The Constitutions or custom

---

[30] Larraona, "Commentarium Codicis," *CpR,* VII (1926), 387.

[31] Schaefer, *De Religiosis,* p. 225; Coronata, *Institutiones,* I, p. 656, n. 538.

[32] Larraona, "Commentarium Codicis," *CpR,* VII (1926), 383, XI; Schaefer, *De Religiosis,* p. 225.

[33] Cf. can. 159: "Every appointment is to be made in writing."

[34] Cf. cans. 177, § 4; 182, § 3; Larraona, "Commentarium Codicis," *CpR,* VII (1926), 388.

[35] Coronata, *Institutiones,* I, p. 657, n. 538.

may provide, or the major superior may declare, that the former superior shall continue to exercise authority. Thus, the former superior would govern as a vicar, or delegate, or vice-superior until the new superior is appointed.[36] If, however, the Constitutions or custom make no such provision for prorogation, and the major superior takes no action, the ruling authority of the community passes to the one who ordinarily takes the place of the absent superior.[37] Canon 505 states that a local superior may be reappointed for a second term of three years if the Constitutions provide for such a reappointment. Papi (1861-1929) believed that, if the Constitutions are silent on this point, a local superior may be reappointed. He maintained that all the Code requires is that the Constitutions *permit* a reappointment, and that this condition is satisfied if they do not forbid it.[38] However, the opposite view seems more in accord with the text of canon 505. The Code does not demand the mere absence of objection on the part of the Constitutions to the reappointment of a local superior. It seems to demand that some positive provision be made by them. Silence on this point cannot be considered as satisfying the condition stated in canon 505: *"si constitutiones ita ferant."*[39] Further support can be added to this argument through a comparison of canon 507, § 3, with canon 505. Canon 507, § 3, allows postulation provided the Constitutions do not *forbid* it: *"dummodo in constitutionibus non prohibeatur."* Canon 505 allows reappointment if the Constitutions *provide* for it: *"si constitutiones ita ferant."* The silence of the Constitutions cannot be construed as *forbidding* postulation, and therefore it is allowed if the Constitutions are silent on this point.[40] However, the silence of the Constitutions can hardly be construed as *providing* for possible reappointment. Therefore, if the Consti-

---

36 Vermeersch-Creusen, *Epitome,* I, p. 462, n. 623; Coronata, *Institutiones,* I, p. 657, n. 538; Schaefer, *De Religiosis,* p. 222, n. 477.

37 Larraona, "Commentarium Codicis," *CpR,* VII (1926), p. 381, nota 202.

38 *The Government of Religious Communities,* p. 72.

39 Cf. Schaefer, *De Religiosis,* p. 222, n. 472; Coronata, *Institutiones,* I, p. 657, n. 538.

40 Cf. supra, p. 64.

tutions make no positive provision for the possible reappointment of a local superior, he cannot be appointed for a second term of office.

The prohibition of canon 505 with reference to a third term of office in the same house is to be understood in its proper context. The Code does not forbid a third appointment as such. It forbids an appointment which immediately follows two continuous three-year terms of office in the same house. Thus the provisions of the Code are not violated if the major superior appoints for a third time a superior who took office during the unexpired term of his predecessor. After completing that unexpired term he was appointed for his first regular three-year term, and then reappointed for a second regular term of three years.[41] His tenure of office indeed extended over more than six years, but there was no appointment to office which followed two complete three-year terms. Such a situation could arise in those Congregations which, for the sake of good order, establish, either by Constitution or by custom, that all local superiors shall begin and end their term of office at the same time, oftentimes on the occasion of the meeting of the provincial or general chapter. If death, resignation, or removal cause a vacancy, the major superior could appoint a subject to complete this term of office. Such a partial term is not to be considered, and in fact is not, the three-year term spoken of in the Code. Thus, although the subject may later be appointed a third time, he is actually being appointed for his second term of three years. The provision of canon 505 is not violated.

Similarly a third appointment is not forbidden if the Constitutions, while allowing such a reappointment to office, determine that the local superior shall hold office for only two years. His third appointment to a two-year term does not run counter to the provisions of canon 505.[42]

---

[41] Schaefer, *De Religiosis,* p. 224, n. 475; Larraona, "Commentarium Codicis," *CpR,* VII (1926), 385; Coronata, *Institutiones,* I, p. 656, n. 538.

[42] Larraona, "Commentarium Codicis," *CpR,* VII (1926), 386.

While it is specified that a subject cannot be reappointed immediately after completing two three-year terms, the common law does not determine what interval of time must elapse before a new appointment to the same office can be made. Hence it seems that the appointment of another superior, even though the new superior hold office for only a short period of time, would constitute an interruption which would satisfy the requirements of canon 505. In such circumstances the major superior could reappoint the previous superior who had already completed two three-year terms.[43] As is evident, such a course of action could not be undertaken in an attempt to circumvent the law.

The superior who has completed two three-year terms cannot without a temporal interruption be appointed to a third term in the same house, but the Code does not prohibit the reappointment of the superior for a third term in another house.[44]

It is reasonable to suppose that the lawgiver would not wish his law to have binding force if it were to cause undue confusion and hardship on religious communities. Thus, during wartime, when communication services become gravely impaired, and it is difficult, if not impossible, for the major superiors to contact their subjects who live in distant countries, the law concerning the restrictive duration in the tenure of the office of local superior would cease to oblige by reason of *epikeia*.[45]

If grave reasons suggest or demand the re-election of a local superior for a third time, then the required procedure becomes that of postulation, provided the conditions of canon 507, § 3, are verified.[46]

---

[43] Fanfani, *De Iure Religiosorum,* p. 89, n. 50, B); De Carlo, *Jus Religiosorum,* p. 48, 5, a).

[44] De Carlo, *Jus Religiosorum,* p. 48, 6; Fanfani, *De Iure Religiosorum,* p. 89, n. 50, B).

[45] Vermeersch-Creusen, *Epitome,* I, n. 623; Schaefer, *De Religiosis,* p. 226, n. 477.

[46] De Carlo, *Jus Religiosorum,* p. 48, n. 67, III, 5, d); Abbo-Hannan, *The Sacred Canons,* I, 515.

The question concerning the loss of office in consequence of the expiration of the term of office of the local superior has already been considered.[47] It remains to treat of the other ways in which the local superior ceases to hold his office, namely, upon resignation, deprivation, removal, transfer, and death.[48]

Canons 184-191, which deal with resignation from an ecclesiastical office, have application, at least by analogy, to the question under consideration. Thus the superior who accepts the resignation of the local superior is any superior who has the right of confirmation, admission or institution.[49] He shall do so only if there be a just and proportionate cause in support of the local superior's desire to be relieved of his office.[50] In order to be valid, the resignation must be made in writing or orally before two witnesses,[51] and made without grave fear, deceit, substantial error, or simony.[52] Once the resignation has been lawfully tendered and accepted, and the incumbent has been notified of the acceptance, the office becomes vacant;[53] the subject shall of course remain in office until he has received reliable notification of the due acceptance of his resignation.[54]

Deprivation is a canonical act by which an office is taken away from an incumbent independently of his consent. Canon 192, § 1, states that deprivation may be effected in virtue of the law itself or by virtue of the action of a legitimate superior. This penal sanction may be attached to the commission of a crime, so that the loss of office is incurred automatically *(latæ sententiæ)*. Thus the local superior who has been declared an *excommunicatus vitandus* automatically forfeits his office.[55] If he becomes a *fugitivus* from the religious life, he automatically

---

[47] Supra, pp. 66-67.

[48] Cf. can. 183, § 1.

[49] Can. 187, § 2.

[50] Can. 189, § 1.

[51] Can. 186.

[52] Can. 185.

[53] Can. 190, § 1.

[54] Can. 190, § 2.

[55] Can. 2266.

incurs the same penalty.[56] The commission of any of the crimes which bring about the automatic dismissal from the religious life would of course also deprive him from his office.[57] In other cases, the loss of office may be dependent on judicial sentence *(ferendæ sententiæ)*.[58] The Constitutions generally determine which superior is competent to act in depriving the local superior of his office, whether his action calls for the previous consultation or consent of his council, and whether the Superior General must also be consulted. Since the Code supposes that the local superior shall hold office with a certain stability, he should not without a just cause be removed by the major superior.[59] Removal from office before the end of the normal term would be justified only in unusual circumstances and for just and serious causes.

Similarly, the Constitutions must be consulted if one is to determine the procedure to be followed in the transferring of a local superior to another position before the term of his office has expired. It is of importance to note in this connection that major superiors and others who have the right to appoint, remove or transfer a local superior must carefully abide by the provisions of the Code concerning the appointment, removal and transfer of pastors, and must see to it that the local ordinary is properly notified if the local superior also holds the office of pastor.[60]

---

[56] Can. 2386.

[57] Cf. can. 646.

[58] E.g., cans., 2331, § 2; 2334; 2335; 2336; 2343, § 1, 1°, § 2, 3°; 2345; 2346; 2347; 2354, § 2; 2359, § 2; 2360, §§ 1, 2; 2389; 2413, §§ 1, 2.

[59] Balmes, *Les Religieux à voeux simples*, p. 61.

[60] Cf. cans. 454, § 5; 456.

CHAPTER V

THE RIGHTS AND DUTIES OF THE LOCAL SUPERIOR

Article 1. The Authority of the Local Superior in Spiritual Matters

One of the first duties of the subject selected for the position of local superior is to make the profession of faith.[1] The local superior is bound to make such a profession because the Church wishes to safeguard the subjects of superiors. It insists that those who are placed in a position of authority declare under oath their profession of the Catholic faith and their freedom from heresy and schism. The superior makes his profession before the religious chapter which elected him, or before the major superior who appointed him, or before the delegate of the chapter or the major superior.

In making his profession of faith, the local superior must fulfill this duty in person; he cannot make use of a proxy.[2] He is furthermore required to use the formula approved by the Holy See.[3] This formula is substantially that which was introduced by Pope Pius IV[4] and later was modified through the additions decreed by the Sacred Congregation of the Council.[5] It now appears at the beginning of the Code of Canon Law.

In addition to the profession of faith made by the local superior, the oath against Modernism must be taken. The taking of this oath was prescribed by Pope Pius X in his *motu proprio Sacrorum antistitum*.[6] Since this disciplinary law which antedated

[1] Cf. can. 1406, § 1, 9°; Balmes, *Les Religieux à voeux simples,* p. 64; Berutti, *Institutiones,* III, p. 65, n. 32, I; Schaefer, *De Religiosis,* p. 265, n. 534.

[2] Can. 1407.

[3] Can. 1406, § 1.

[4] Const. *Iniunctum nobis,* 13 nov. 1564 — *Fontes,* n. 108.

[5] 20 ian. 1877 — *Acta Sanctae Sedis* (41 vols., Romae, 1865-1908), X (1877), 74.

[6] 1 sept. 1910 — *Fontes,* n. 689.

the Code was not included, even implicitly, in the Code, it would ordinarily have lost all force.[7] However, a decision of the Holy Office on March 22, 1918, declared that the obligation of taking this oath continues in force until the Holy See provides otherwise.[8] The local superior is at present, therefore, obliged to take the oath against Modernism. He takes this before the major superior or his delegate.[9]

The profession of faith and the oath against Modernism must be repeated whenever the local superior, giving up a previous appointment, obtains a new office, even if the new office is of the same species as the old.[10] Thus if the local superior at the end of his three-year term is reappointed to the same office even in the same house, he is bound to repeat his profession of faith and the oath against Modernism.[11] If he is transferred from the office of superior in one house to a similar office in another house the profession and oath must be taken again.[12]

It will be useful to consider here the procedure to be followed when a religious is appointed simultaneously to two or more compatible offices when to each of them is attached the obligation of making the profession of faith. For example, the subject may, at the same time, be appointed to the office of pastor and to the office of local superior of the community.[13]

---

[7] Cf. can. 6, 6°.

[8] *AAS,* X (1918), 136.

[9] Vermeersch, "Annotationes," *Periodica,* V (1911), 232.

[10] Can. 1406, § 2.

[11] Balmes, *Les Religieux à voeux simples,* pp. 64-65.

[12] Walter Canavan, *The Profession of Faith,* The Catholic University of America Canon Law Studies, n. 151 (Washington, D.C.: The Catholic University of America Press, 1942), 101.

[13] Some canonists maintain that under normal conditions the law insists on the appointment of separate individuals to the two offices of local superior and pastor. Bastnagel states that the incompatibility of these two offices would result from the fact that the same person could not over a sustained period of time fulfill the obligations that attach to the two offices. ("Cases and Studies," *The Jurist,* X (1950), 54, and footnote n. 3; cf. Clancy, *The Local Religious Superior,* pp. 108-109, footnote n. 232.) However, the fact that the approved Constitutions and the corresponding practice of some religious Institutes allow the appointment of the

Each of these offices requires that the profession of faith be made.[14] Must the subject make two professions, one before the local ordinary or his delegate and one before his religious superior, or will one profession suffice? Canavan states, "according to a declaration of the Sacred Consistorial Congregation, the obligation can be satisfied by one and the same profession of faith *if the person before whom the profession of faith must be made is the same person, e.g., the local Ordinary*.[15] If the persons to whom the profession of faith must be made are distinct, e.g., the religious chapter and the local Ordinary in the case of one who is at the same time nominated a religious superior and appointed a pastor of a parish, two professions of faith must be made by that person."[16] Canavan cites the authority of the declaration of the Sacred Consistorial Congregation dated October 25, 1910.[17] and refers to the statements of Coronata[18] and Vermeersch.[19] However, an examination of the *dubium* proposed to the Sacred Consistorial Congregation and the reply given does not substantiate the explanation given by Canavan. The Sacred Congregation did not state that one profession of faith would suffice only in the cases in which "the person before whom the profession of faith must be made is the same person." It stated that one profession would suffice, but that a testimonial proving that it was so taken was to be shown to the person who would otherwise have the right to demand that it be taken again.[20] Canavan's explanation

---

same individual for the two offices of local superior and pastor lets one conclude with assurance that the two offices are not intrinsically or inherently incompatible in relation to each other.

14 Can. 1406, § 1, 7°, 8°.

15 Italics added.

16 *The Profession of Faith*, p. 101.

17 *AAS*, II (1910), 856-857.

18 *Institutiones*, II, 352.

19 "Annotationes," *Periodica*, V (1911), 232.

20 S. C. Const., 25 oct. 1910, *AAS*, II (1910), 856-857: "I. Utrum qui, in praesenti, plura obtinent officia vel beneficia, unum dumtaxat iusiurandum praestare possint, an tot iuramenta emittere teneantur quot possident officia vel beneficia; . . . Ad I. Sufficere unum iusiurandum, sed de eodem prius praestito fides exibenda est ei, qui ius habet aliud exigendi iuramentum."

agrees with that of Vermeersch.[21] The other author cited, Coronata,[22] merely repeats and refers to Vermeersch's view. It is of interest, however, to note that Vermeersch expressed his views on this question in "Annotationes" to a previous declaration of the Sacred Consistorial Congregation dated Sept. 25, 1910.[23] As Vermeersch noted, no solution to the problem under consideration was contained in this earlier declaration.[24] The official answer given on October 25, 1910, explicitly provides a solution more liberal than the one proposed by Vermeersch. It is safe to assert, therefore, that if a religious subject is simultaneously appointed as local superior and as pastor, he need make only one profession of faith and oath against Modernism. However, a testimonial proving that he has done so must be shown to the person who would otherwise have the right to demand the making of a second profession or the taking of the oath a second time.

If without a legitimate excuse the local superior has neglected to make the profession of faith, he is to be admonished by his major superior to do so within a specified period of time. If he stubbornly persists in his refusal beyond the term fixed, he shall be punished even with deprivation of office.[25] The penalties for neglect of the profession of faith do not apply to the local superior's neglect of the anti-Modernist oath.[26] Those, however, who violate this oath are to be reported to the Holy Office.[27]

The local superior is entrusted with the responsibility of directing and guiding his subjects in their quest for spiritual perfection.[28] This obligation demands that he live in the house that has been committed to his care.[29] While it is true that the obliga-

---

21 "Annotationes," *Periodica*, V (1911), 232.

22 *Institutiones*, II, 352.

23 *AAS*, II (1910), 740-741.

24 Cf. Vermeersch, "Annotationes," *Periodica*, V (1911), 232.

25 Cf. can. 2403; Canavan, *The Profession of Faith*, pp. 104-110.

26 Vermeersch-Creusen, *Epitome*, III, 376.

27 Motu prop. *Sacrorum antistitum*, 1 sept. 1910 — *AAS*, II (1910), 669.

28 Cf. Balmes, *Les Religieux à voeux simples*, p. 65.

29 Can. 508.

tion of maintaining residence is incumbent on all religious superiors, the law applies especially to local superiors.[30] Major superiors may often be legitimately absent from their place of residence in line with the official responsibilities of their office.[31] However, delinquency in the matter of residence on the part of the local superior can easily give rise to numerous and grievous evils.[32] The Code does not specify for the local superior, as it does in the case of the bishop[33] and the pastor,[34] the duration of lawful absences. Such specifications are to be determined by the individual Constitutions. They generally determine not only the length of the absence but also the circumstances or causes which may justify such absence.

The Constitutions should designate the religious who is to take the superior's place while he is away. In the absence of such a provision the superior is to provide for the continuous and harmonious government of his house by appointing and instructing a substitute. If the local superior holds the office of pastor he must, of course, observe the law concerning the appointment of a substitute according to the provisions of canon 465, §§ 4, 5, 6.

Violations of the law of residence are not strictly and properly violations of the obligation of the common life.[35] Hence they are not directly subject to the penalties imposed by canon 2389 for violations of the common life.[36] Such violations of the law of residence can, nevertheless, be punished by the major superiors, even to the extent of removal from office. Such action

[30] Fanfani, *De Iure Religiosorum*, p. 181, n. 125, A); De Carlo, *Jus Religiosorum*, p. 55, n. 75; Abbo-Hannan, *The Sacred Canons*, I, p. 518, n. 508.

[31] Cf. can. 511.

[32] Berutti, *Institutiones*, III, p. 63, n. 32, II.

[33] Can. 338.

[34] Can. 465.

[35] Mariner Smith, *The Penal Law for Religious*, The Catholic University of America Canon Law Studies, n. 98 (Washington, D.C.: The Catholic University of America, 1935), p. 124, footnote 4; Clancy, *The Local Religious Superior*, p. 58.

[36] Clancy, *The Local Religious Superior*, p. 58.

of course would not be of a judicial nature, since the major superior in a non-exempt Congregation does not possess jurisdiction by the common law.[37] It would amount to a removal, and indeed for a good cause, as exercised by the major superior empowered to do so by the Constitutions. If the local superior who has seriously neglected the law of residence is also a pastor, the local ordinary could also take action against him in regard to his parish. The ordinary would not, however, proceed according to the provisions of canon 2381, which applies not to religious but only to clerics as such.[38] Nor would he punish the delinquent with an administrative removal from his office according to the norm of canons 2168-2175. These canons deal with the manner of proceeding against *clerics* who violate the laws of residence, and do not apply to *religious.*[39] Pastors who belong to a religious community are always, as far as the individual person is concerned, removable *ad nutum.* They may be removed by the local ordinary, who of course in accordance with the law must send a report of this act of removal to the religious superior.[40] Therefore a local ordinary who considers that a religious pastor has seriously violated the law of residence could simply remove him from the office of pastor and notify his religious superior.

The Code wisely provides that the local superior have aides in his task of caring for the spiritual and temporal welfare of his subjects. In every completely organized house the local superior must have councillors whose consent or advice is to be sought in accordance with the Constitutions and the Sacred Canons.[41] But the local superior of a house that is only partially organized may also have his council.[42] It is of importance to note that the

---

[37] Cf. can. 501, § 1.

[38] Berutti, *Institutiones,* III, p. 65, n. 32, II; De Carlo, *Jus Religiosorum,* p. 55, n. 75; Schaefer, *De Religiosis,* p. 266, n. 535.

[39] Schaefer, *De Religiosis,* p. 266, n. 535.

[40] Can. 454, § 5.

[41] Can. 516, § 1.

[42] Schaefer, *De Religiosis,* p. 295, n. 578; Abbo-Hannan, *The Sacred Canons,* I, p. 526, n. 516.

authority in the house resides in the superior. The council has no power of government.[43] The council can, however, prevent the superior from acting validly when their consent is demanded by the Code. If they refuse to give it, the superior cannot act validly.[44] However, the council cannot force the superior to act.[45]

The superior must avoid two extremes in his dealings with his councillors. He would be guilty of dangerous presumption were he to attempt to decide all matters himself without consulting his council. On the other hand, he would be guilty of cowardly renunciation of authority if he were to throw all responsibility for his decisions back on his council.[46] The Code demands that the superior be assisted by councillors as an aid to good government. The local superior should work with them to attain that end.

The obligations imposed on superiors by canon 595 with reference to the exercises of piety of their subjects have direct reference to the local superior. The fulfillment of these obligations will be all the easier if the local superior by his own faithful and regular practice of the exercises demanded by the Code sets an example for his subjects. His leadership in these matters will be a source of inspiration and encouragement for his subjects.[47]

While canon 595, §1, 1°, demands that the local superior must take care that his subjects make a retreat every year, it

---

[43] Goyeneche, "Consultationes," *CpRM*, XI (1930), 350; Vermeersch, "De consiliariis superiorum," *Periodica*, XV (1926), pp. (61)-(63).

[44] Cf. can. 105, 1°. The Holy See has not authentically decided the celebrated dispute among canonists concerning the value of acts performed by a superior who neglects to *consult* his councillors in cases in which mere consultation is demanded. Since the view upholding their validity has at least extrinsic probability, such acts need not be considered invalid. Cf. Schaefer, *De Religiosis*, p. 296, n. 581; Abbo-Hannan, *The Sacred Canons*, I, 153-154.

[45] Heston, "Some Aspects of Government in Religious Communities," *The Jurist*, X (1950), 49.

[46] Heston, "Some Aspects of Government in Religious Communities," *The Jurist*, X (1950), pp. 50-51.

[47] Cf. Berutti, *Institutiones*, III, p. 251, n. 110, c).

does not specify the length of such a retreat nor the circumstances under which it is to be made. Such determinations are left to the Constitutions or legitimate custom. If they be silent, the superior may make his own regulations.[48] In this connection the superior could with profit consult the encyclical *Mens nostra* of Pope Pius XI.[49]

Unless the subject is lawfully prevented, the local superior should see to it that he assists at Mass every day. The superior should further see to it that his subjects meditate daily[50] according to the directions contained in the Constitutions of the Institute. The general obligation of the local superior to insure observance by his subjects of all the rules and customs of the Institute is specified in canon 595. It insists that he take care that his subjects assiduously perform all the spiritual exercises prescribed by the Rules and Constitutions.[51] Many Constitutions, for example, prescribe a daily visit to the Blessed Sacrament, recitation of the rosary, two periods of meditation and examination of conscience. The local superior is bound to see that all the prescribed exercises are faithfully carried out.

In fulfilling his obligation to see that each of his subjects goes to confession once a week,[52] the local superior should provide ample opportunity for his subjects to approach the designated confessors mentioned in canon 518, § 1. He should furthermore provide them with the opportunity of making a confession shortly before the time of Communion.[53] If the superior believes that one of his subjects is lax in fulfilling his obligation of weekly confession, he is quite within his rights to ask the subject whether he is going to confession each week, and where, and when.[54] But he cannot interrogate his subject concerning

[48] De Carlo, *Jus Religiosorum*, p. 290, n. 348; Coronata, *Institutiones*, I, p. 793, n. 608.

[49] 20 dec. 1929 — *AAS*, XXI (1930), 689.

[50] Can. 595, § 1, 2°.

[51] Cf. can. 595, § 1, 2°.

[52] Can. 595, § 1, 3°.

[53] S. C. de Sacramentis, 8 dec. 1938 — Bouscaren, *The Canon Law Digest*, II, p. 210, n. 2.

[54] Schaefer, *De Religiosis*, p. 677, n. 1143.

the extraordinary confessions made to a confessor not designated by the superior.[55] Freedom is allowed to a religious subject by canon 519 to quiet his conscience by going to confession to any confessor approved by the local ordinary. The local superior cannot take away this right. The Code expects the local superior to urge rather than force his subjects to go to confession.[56] He should not manifest unwarranted suspicion or impose odious systems of control.[57] He should rather exhort and encourage his subjects to make frequent use of this most salutary means of sanctification.

The local superior himself, provided he has the required faculties, can hear the confessions of his subjects when they spontaneously and voluntarily approach him for this purpose. But he shall not make a habit of this without a grave justifying reason.[58] He must avoid inducing his subjects to confess to him through the use, either in person or through others, of force, fear, importunate recommendations or other means.[59] The Code does not demand the existence of a grave reason if the subject wishes to confess to his superior occasionally. However, if the subject habitually makes his confession to his superior, there must be present some grave justifying cause in order to render such a practice lawful. Such causes would be, for example, the age or ill health of a subject who could confess to another only with some difficulty, or the difficulty in choosing an experienced confessor by someone who has long been accustomed to confess to the one recently appointed as local superior.[60] Other justifying causes would be the emotional difficulty experienced in confessing to other available priests, or the handicap of language.[61]

---

[55] Vermeersch-Creusen, *Epitome,* I, p. 566, n. 75; Abbo-Hannan, *The Sacred Canons,* 1, p. 619, n. 595; Schaefer, *De Religiosis,* p. 677, n. 1143.

[56] Beste, *Introductio in Codicem,* p. 410; Schaefer, *De Religiosis,* p. 676, n. 1143.

[57] Abbo-Hannan, *The Sacred Canons,* I, p. 619, n. 595, 3°.

[58] Can. 518, § 2.

[59] Can. 518, § 3.

[60] Berutti, *Institutiones,* III, 78.

[61] Abbo-Hannan, *The Sacred Canons,* I, p. 529, n. 518, 2.

Closely allied with the regulations concerning the superior's power to hear the confessions of his subjects is the regulation concerning the manifestation of conscience outside confession. The local superior is strictly forbidden to induce his subjects by any means whatever to manifest their conscience to him.[62] This is a grave precept, although it does allow of parvity of matter.[63] The superior cannot resort to precept, counsel, intimidation, threats or flattery to induce the subjects to make such a manifestation.[64]

Taken in its narrower and proper sense, manifestation of conscience includes such things as the revelation of one's virtues or faults, temptations, doubts or anxieties, and such revelations in general as are usually reserved to the confessional.[65] The superior cannot inquire about such matters nor can he demand that the subject speak of them. In its wider meaning, manifestation of conscience extends to such things as counsel, instruction, and exhortation concerning various aspects of the spiritual life. It includes instruction on points of the Rule, e.g., the methods to be followed in prayer, the practice of meditation or examination of conscience or other exercises of piety. The superior may question his subjects concerning these matters in order to offer them salutary advice and direction.[66] The prohibition of demanding a manifestation of conscience does not extend to the faults and failings of the subjects which have become externalized. The superior is certainly allowed to question, correct, and even punish his subjects concerning their external violations of the Rule and discipline of the house, especially if these matters have become noticeable to others and are a cause of scandal.[67]

---

[62] Can. 530, § 1.

[63] Beste, *Introductio in Codicem,* p. 354.

[64] S. C. Ep. et Reg., 17 dec. 1890, n. 2 — *Fontes,* n. 2017.

[65] Beste, *Introductio in Codicem,* p. 354; Nicholas Gill, *The Spiritual Prefect in Clerical Religious Houses of Study,* The Catholic University of America Canon Law Studies, n. 216 (Washington, D.C.: The Catholic University of America Press, 1945), p. 98.

[66] Beste, *Introductio in Codicem,* p. 354.

[67] Berutti, *Institutiones,* III, 109, B; Schaefer, *De Religiosis,* p. 367, n. 690.

The superior, motivated by charity, may most prudently inquire into the reasons for the sadness or anxiety manifested by one of his subjects.[68] But he may not insist that the subject reveal his inmost feelings. He should rather suggest to his subject that the advice of a prudent confessor be sought.

Any manifestation of conscience which the subject freely makes to his local superior should be cheerfully and readily received. Subjects are not forbidden to open their hearts freely and voluntarily to their superior. Indeed, the Code states that it is expedient that they should approach him with filial confidence.[69] The local superior who rejects such a manifestation of conscience without a sufficient cause acts imprudently and uncharitably.[70]

The local superior should promote among his subjects frequent, even daily, reception of Holy Communion. Opportunity should be granted to all properly disposed religious to receive Holy Communion frequently, even daily.[71] The superior, however, may not command his subjects to receive Communion, nor can he forbid them to do so except in the case discussed below.[72] Such decisions are to be left to the subject's confessor.[73]

The Sacred Congregation of the Sacraments on December 8, 1938, issued a reserved Instruction on the daily reception of Holy Communion and the precautions to be taken against abuses.[74] The local superior should be fully cognizant of the contents of this important document and should strive to enforce each of its provisions and directives.

---

[68] Joseph Creusen, *Religious Men and Women in the Code* (3. English ed. revised and edited to conform with 5. French ed. by Adam Ellis; first translation by Edward Garesché, Milwaukee: The Bruce Publishing Company, 1940), p. 98, n. 131 (hereinafter cited as *Religious*).

[69] Can. 530, § 2.

[70] Creusen, *Religious*, p. 99, n. 132.

[71] Can. 595, § 2.

[72] Cf. *infra*, p. 83.

[73] Fanfani, *De Iure Religiosorum*, p. 477, n. 323, B); Beste, *Introductio in Codicem*, p. 410.

[74] Bouscaren, *The Canon Law Digest*, II, 508-515.

A superior can forbid his subject to receive Holy Communion if, subsequent to his latest confession, he has given grave scandal to the community or committed a serious external offense.[75] Schaefer († 1948) stated that the superior's power to forbid the reception of Holy Communion is limited to cases involving grave external theological fault. He based his interpretation on the principle, *odia sunt restringenda.* He also indicated that canon 901 requires the confession of only mortal sins, and therefore the superior cannot oblige his subject to make a confession of what is venially sinful.[76]

Such a conclusion would be warranted if the purpose of canon 595, § 3, were penal. However, it seems more correct to say that the purpose of this canon is principally disciplinary.[77] The superior's action is directed to the preservation of good discipline in the community rather than to the punishment of his subject. Exception can also be taken to Schaefer's view because the law authorizes the superior to forbid the reception of Holy Communion in the event that grave scandal has been given, *or* a serious external fault has been committed. The two cases are not necessarily connected. Drunkenness, for example, if it is inculpable, does not involve serious sin, and yet it may be the cause of grave scandal to the community. Striking a superior or a co-religious might be grievously sinful, and yet if done privately it may not cause grave scandal. In each case the superior would be entitled to forbid the reception of Holy Communion until the subject has once more approached the sacrament of penance.[78] This interpretation, in the opinion of the writer, seems to be more in accord with the text and meaning of the law.

Every local superior is obliged to promote the observance of the regulations of canon 595. It is to be noted, however, that

---

[75] Can. 595, § 3.

[76] *De Religiosis,* p. 678, n. 1145.

[77] Clancy, *The Local Religious Superior,* p. 99.

[78] Beste, *Introductio in Codicem,* p. 410; Vermeersch-Creusen, *Epitome,* I, p. 567, n. 751, § 3; Augustine, *Commentary,* III, 308-309.

the local superior in a house of studies is required to insist that the provisions of canon 595 affecting religious life are observed perfectly in his house.[79]

The knowledge and observance of the decrees of the Holy See pertaining to religious are to be promoted by the local superior.[80] The decrees which deal with the obligations of the religious life are not the only ones the knowledge of which is useful and sometimes necessary to the members of the community. Among the responses or instructions given by the Sacred Congregations concerning pious associations, indulgences, and the liturgy are to be found decisions which have immediate interest for the superior's subjects.[81] Furthermore, it is in keeping with the spirit of canon 509, § 1, if the local superior arranges for the regular public reading of those sections of the Code which deal with religious.[82] Familiarity with the contents of the current issues of the *Acta Apostolicæ Sedis* will aid the local superior in his fulfillment of these obligations.

At least once a year the local superior is to make provision for the public reading of the Constitutions of his Institute.[83] The time and place for such reading is determined by the Constitutions themselves or by custom and the practice of the community.[84] If the Constitutions are very long, the reading of an approved summary of the matters which have reference to all the members may be substituted for the reading of the complete Constitutions.[85] In the opinion of the writer, it seems that in order to allow the reading of such summaries in place of the reading of the whole Constitutions, the summaries must have been accorded a due approval either in the Constitutions or

[79] Cf. can. 588, § 3.

[80] Can. 509, § 1.

[81] Creusen, *Religious,* p. 62, n. 86.

[82] Coronata, *Institutiones,* I, p. 664, n. 540, b); Augustine, *Commentary,* III, 131; Schaefer, *De Religiosis,* p. 268, n. 537.

[83] Can. 509, § 2, 1°.

[84] Schaefer, *De Religiosis,* pp. 267-268, n. 537.

[85] Vermeersch-Creusen, *Epitome,* I, p. 467, n. 628, 4; De Carlo, *Jus Religiosorum,* p. 56, n. 76, II; Creusen, *Religious,* p. 62, n. 86.

through legitimate custom, or their use must have been permitted by Apostolic indult.

The superior is also obliged to provide for the annual reading of the decrees which the Holy See orders to be read in public.[86] At the present time, the Holy See has prescribed the reading of only one decree. It is the Instruction issued by the Sacred Congregation for Religious concerning the training of candidates for the priesthood. It is to be read publicly at the beginning of each year in the houses of study of religious clerics.[87]

The obligation of providing an instruction in Christian doctrine twice a month for lay brothers and for members of the household *(familiares)* rests with the local superior.[88] The term "lay brothers" *(conversi)* may be defined as designating a second, non-clerical group of religious devoted *ex professo* to manual labor in clerical communities admitting this additional class.[89]

Authors are not in agreement as to the extension of the term "members of the household" *(familiares)*. Some would restrict its meaning so that the local superior would be required to give instruction in Christian doctrine only to lay brothers and to those who are domestic servants residing day and night in the religious house.[90] Others hold the view, which to the present writer seems more probable, that the term *familiares* as used in canon 509, § 2, 2°, includes all the persons listed in canon 514, § 1. [91] According to this view, the local superior is bound

---

[86] Can. 509, § 2, 1°.

[87] 1 dec. 1931 — *AAS,* XXIV (1932), 74-81. Cf. Bouscaren, *The Canon Law Digest,* I, 473-482.

[88] Can. 509, § 2, 2°.

[89] Cf. Thomas Aquinas Brockhaus, *Religious Who are Known as Conversi,* The Catholic University of America Canon Law Studies, n. 225 (Washington, D.C.: The Catholic University of America Press, 1946), p. 57.

[90] Fanfani, *De Iure Religiosorum,* p. 600, n. 441, A); Vermeersch-Creusen, *Epitome,* I, p. 467, n. 629, 5; Schaefer, *De Religiosis,* p. 268, n. 539.

[91] Brys, *Juris Canonici Compendium,* I, p. 512, nota 2; Coronata, *Institutiones,* I, 665; De Carlo, *Jus Religiosorum,* p. 57, n. 76 bis, 4; Beste, *Introductio in Codicem,* p. 339; Abbo-Hannan, *The Sacred Canons,* I, p. 519, n. 509, 2°.

to provide instruction for those who dwell day and night in the religious house by reason of domestic service, education, hospitality or for the purpose of recovering their health. The superior is authorized to administer the last sacraments to these persons[92] because of their intimate connection with the religious community. It seems reasonable to conclude that the legislator expects the superior to look out for their spiritual welfare by providing for their Christian instruction during their lifetime.

Besides this instruction in Christian doctrine a pious exhortation at least twice a month to all the members of the community should be arranged for by the local superior in accord with the law expressed in canon 509, § 2, 2°. Some authors maintain that this canon does not require such exhortation in clerical Institutes,[93] or at least that the obligation to have them in clerical Institutes is not a grave one.[94] Such conclusions do not seem warranted from the wording of the text of the canon. The Code states that the local superior is to see that such exhortations be given. The canon insists *(præsertim)* that they be given in lay Institutes. Had the law-giver wished to make the giving of these exhortations obligatory only in lay Institutes, he could have omitted the word *præsertim.* Its inclusion in the law emphasizes the requirement of these exhorations in lay Institutes, but leaves intact the demand that they be given in all Institutes.

Canon 509, § 2, demands that the pious exhortation be given *"ad omnes de familia."* There is general agreement among the authors as to the meaning of the phrase, *"ad omnes de familia."* It means that the exhortation is to be given to the members of the Institute, inclusive of the novices but exclusive of the domestic servants and guests.[95]

---

[92] Can. 514, § 1.

[93] Augustine, *Commentary,* III, 131.

[94] Schaefer, *De Religiosis,* p. 266, n. 539; Coronata, *Institutiones,* I, p. 665, n. 540, c).

[95] Brys, *Juris Canonici Compendium,* I, 512, nota 3; F. Claeys Bouuaert — G. Simenon, *Manuale Juris Canonici* (3 vols., Vol. I, 5. ed., Gandae et Leodii: Prostat apud auctores in Seminariis Ganavensi et Leodiensi, 1939), I, 359, IV; Vermeersch-Creusen, *Epitome,* I, p. 468, n.

The catechetical instruction and the pious exhortation are in themselves distinct one from the other, but they may be given together provided that they are accommodated to the needs of the listeners.[96] The superior need not personally fulfill this office, for he can depute it to another priest.[97]

In at least every completely organized house of a clerical religious Institute, there are to be held not less frequently than once a month conferences in which a moral and a liturgical case is solved. At the direction of the superior, a sermon is delivered on dogmatic and kindred subjects. Unless the Constitutions provide otherwise, attendance at such conferences is required for all professed clerics residing in the house if they are students of theology, or have finished their theological studies.[98] The responsibility for seeing that these conferences are held regularly as prescribed rests with the local superior. He may, however, delegate some competent priest to preside. The Code allows the Constitutions to make exceptions regarding the prescriptions of canon 591, which indicates which religious are to attend. If the Constitutions are silent on this point, the superior should be guided by the prescriptions of the present canon.[99] Custom seems to permit the omission of these conferences during the two or three months of summer vacation.[100]

Earlier in this chapter the rights and obligations of the local superior with reference to the reception by his subjects of the

629; De Carlo, *Jus Religiosorum,* p. 57, n. 76 bis, 6; Schaefer, *De Religiosis,* p. 269, n. 539; Beste, *Introductio in Codicem,* p. 339; Fanfani, *De Iure Religiosorum,* p. 600, n. 441, B); Abbo-Hannan, *The Sacred Canons,* I, p. 519, n. 509, § 2, 2°.

[96] Vermeersch-Creusen, *Epitome,* I, p. 467, n. 629, 5; Beste, *Introductio in Codicem,* p. 339; Schaefer, *De Religiosis,* pp. 268-269, n. 539.

[97] Fanfani, *De Iure Religiosorum,* p. 600, n. 441, B); Vermeersch-Creusen, *Epitome,* I, p. 467, n. 629, 5.

[98] Can. 591.

[99] Cf. Schaefer, *De Religiosis,* p. 622, n. 1044.

[100] Augustine, *Commentary,* III, 297; Beste, *Introductio in Codicem,* p. 408; Vermeersch-Creusen, *Epitome,* I, p. 558, n. 744, 2.

sacraments of penance[101] and the Holy Eucharist,[102] and their assistance at daily Mass were discussed.[103] The superior's rights and duties in connection with the celebration of Mass will now be considered. To this will be added a discussion of his rights concerning the administration of the last sacraments and the granting of ecclesiastical burial.

The Code contains no precept whereby the local superior is bound to offer the Sacrifice of the Mass for his subjects. However, it seems most fitting, in charity, that he should sometimes do so.[104]

The local superior is to see to it that those of his subjects who are priests celebrate Mass at least on Sundays and on other holy days of obligation.[105] However, he should exhort and admonish his subjects in this regard rather than command them.[106] He will of course encourage them to celebrate Mass frequently, even daily.

Supervision over the fulfillment of the obligations connected with Mass stipends belongs to the superiors of religious in the churches of religious.[107] The local superior who entrusts the celebration of Masses to his subjects or to others must promptly record in a book, in proper order, the stipends he has received, together with the amount offered. He should exert every effort to see that the Masses are celebrated as soon as possible.[108] The local superior should be well acquainted with the provisions of canons 824-841 concerning the acceptance, custody, fulfillment and distribution of stipends.

---

[101] Cf. *supra,* pp. 79-80.

[102] Cf. *supra,* pp. 82-83.

[103] Cf. *supra,* p. 79.

[104] Cf. Thomas Donnellan, *The Obligation of the Missa pro Populo,* The Catholic University of America Canon Law Series, n. 155 (Washington, D.C.: The Catholic University of America Press, 1942), pp. 60-61; De Carlo, *Jus Religiosorum,* p. 390, n. 461, II.

[105] Can. 805.

[106] Abbo-Hannan, *The Sacred Canons,* I, 798-799.

[107] Can. 842.

[108] Can. 844, § 1.

The Code requires a priest religious to obtain his celebret from his superior.[109] The celebret is the popular name for the commendatory letter which will obtain for a priest admission to the celebration of Mass in a church other than the one to which he is attached. The competence of the local superior to issue a celebret to his priest subjects has been well established.[110] The local superior is required to examine diligently the celebrets exhibited by unknown priests. Only if the conditions set down in canon 804 are verified may he admit outside priests to celebrate Mass in his church or oratory.[111]

In every clerical Institute the local superior is the proper person to administer Holy Viaticum and Extreme Unction in case of illness to the professed, the novices, and others who live day and night in the religious house by reason of services to be rendered, education to be received, hospitality to be shared, or health to be recovered.[112] Postulants, though not specifically mentioned in canon 514, § 1, are to be included in the group of those to whom the local superior may administer these sacraments, because they pertain at least to the *familiares* who dwell in the religious house.[113]

The term *"diu noctuque"* seems to indicate a certain permanence of residence extending over a number of days and nights. Since we are concerned here with the care of the sick, a more liberal interpretation allows the local superior to administer to those who reside in the religious house for a period of 24 hours.[114] The superior may administer the last sacraments

---

[109] Can. 804, § 1.

[110] George Schorr, *The Law of the Celebret,* The Catholic University of America Canon Law Studies, n. 332 (Washington, D.C.: The Catholic University of America Press, 1952), pp. 53-55; Pejska, *Ius Canonicum,* p. 264.

[111] Schorr, *The Law of the Celebret,* pp. 74-83.

[112] Can. 514, § 1.

[113] Pejska, *Ius Canonicum,* p. 87; Schaefer, *De Religiosis,* p. 236, n. 565; Fanfani, *De Iure Religiosorum,* p. 573, n. 415; Berutti, *Institutiones,* III, p. 54, n. 27, A).

[114] Coronata, *Institutiones,* I, 669; Augustine, *Commentary,* III, 142, (2); Abbo-Hannan, *The Sacred Canons,* I, 524.

even to those who take up residence in the religious house with the intention of staying for at least a full day or more.[115]

Residence in the religious house implies that one lives on the premises of the foundation or *intra septa monasterii.*[116] A number of buildings may be understood as constituting one "religious house", provided they are owned by the religious and are within the precincts of the religious property. Thus, a school, or house for employees, if morally contiguous with the religious establishment, would fulfill such requirements.[117] According to canon 514, § 1, the local superior is authorized to administer the last sacraments to those who reside in such buildings. This same power may be exercised for the benefit of the residents of a filial house canonically dependent on this superior, even though it is not *intra septa monasterii.*[118]

Even when the professed members of the community and the novices are outside the religious house, the local superior may administer the last sacraments to them without having to seek the permission of the pastor. When, however, the servants, students, guests and the infirm are outside the religious house, the right to administer Holy Viaticum and Extreme Unction to them reverts to the pastor. The superior needs at least the presumed permission of the pastor or of the local ordinary before he can administer these sacraments.[119]

An examination of the rights of the local superior in connection with ecclesiastical burial requires a treatment of the different classes of persons mentioned in canons 1121 and 1122. These are the professed religious, novices, servants, and guests,

---

[115] De Carlo, *Jus Religiosorum,* p. 405, n. 477; Berutti, *Institutiones,* III, p. 54, n. 27, A); Beste, *Introductio in Codicem,* p. 341; Schaefer, *De Religiosis,* p. 286, n. 566.

[116] Augustine, *Commentary,* III, 142, (2).

[117] Coronata, *Institutiones,* I, 669-670; Schaefer, *De Religiosis,* p. 287, n. 567.

[118] Larraona, "Commentarium Codicis," *CpR,* IX (1928), 105, 4°; Coronata, *Institutiones,* I, 670.

[119] Cf. *PCI,* 16 iun. 1931 — *AAS,* XXIII (1931), 353; Bouscaren, *The Canon Law Digest,* I, 294.

students, or patients. In addition, it is necessary to deal with his rights in relation to the burial services of postulants and of the faithful who request to be buried from the religious church.

A professed religious shall at his death be transferred for his funeral to the church or oratory of the house to which he belonged, or at least to one belonging to his Institute.[120] The local superior is authorized to say the liturgical prayers when the body is removed from the place of death, and to accompany it to the church from which the burial is to follow.[121] He is furthermore authorized to conduct the funeral service in the church[122] and to transport the body to the grave.[123]

If the professed religious died at a place so far distant from the house to which he belonged that the body cannot easily be brought to it, or at least to a house of his Institute, the funeral services are to be conducted in the church of the parish in which he died.[124] In this case, the parish priest conducts the funeral services in his parish church.[125] The local superior, however, retains the right of transferring the body of the religious to the religious house.[126] If this is done, then the local superior conducts all the funeral rites.[127]

A novice is allowed to choose the church of his funeral and the cemetery of his burial.[128] If he has made no such choice, the superior's rights regarding his funeral service are the same as those he has with reference to the professed religious, whether

---

120 Can. 1221, § 1.

121 Can. 1221, § 1.

122 Joseph Hale, *The Pastor of Burial,* The Catholic University of America Canon Law Studies, n. 234 (Washington, D.C.: The Catholic University of America Press, 1949), p. 157, V; Coronata, *Institutiones,* II, p. 116, n. 805, e).

123 Can. 1231, § 2.

124 Can. 1221, § 2.

125 Hale, *The Pastor of Burial,* p. 183; Larraona, "Commentarium Codicis," *CpR,* IX (1928), 209; Schaefer, *De Religiosis,* p. 825, n. 1383.

126 Can. 1218, § 3.

127 Can. 1221, § 2.

128 Cans. 1223, 1224.

the novice died inside, or outside, or far distant from the religious house.[129] If the novice has legitimately chosen a church of burial according to the norms of canons 1225-1228, the local superior may remove the body from the place of death and accompany it to the church of the funeral.[130] If the funeral is held in a church of the religious Institute, the local superior conducts the exequies. If, however, the novice had selected another church, the pastor of this church conducts the funeral services.[131]

What has been said concerning the rights of the local superior in reference to the funeral of novices applies to those who were actually in the service of the religious. The superior may conduct the funeral services of such servants if they resided permanently within the premises of the religious house and died there.[132] If the servant died outside the religious house, the funeral should be from the parish church of his domicile or quasi-domicile, whichever is closer, and he is to be buried according to the norms of canons 1216-1218.[133] The church of the religious where the servant was employed is not to be his funeral church if he died outside the religious house, unless the religious church is also his parish church or unless he has legitimately selected it.[134]

In the absence of a particular law or privilege, the local superior is not authorized to conduct the funeral services of guests, students, or patients who died in the religious house or in a college conducted by the religious. The funeral rites of such persons are governed according to the usual norms which regulate the funerals of the faithful.[135]

Similarly, the local superior does not have the right by the common law to conduct the funerals of postulants. Their funerals are not governed by the norms of canon 1221 concerning the

---

129 Can. 1221, §§ 1, 2.

130 Can. 1221, § 1.

131 Hale, *The Pastor of Burial,* p. 183.

132 Can. 1221, § 3.

133 Can. 1221, § 3.

134 Hale, *The Pastor of Burial,* p. 135.

135 Cf. cans. 1222; 1216-1218.

funerals of the professed, the novices and the servants.[136] The funerals of postulants are regulated by the norms which govern the funerals of the faithful.

If a lay person should choose the church of the religious Institute as the church of his funeral, the local pastor, and not the local superior, has the right to conduct the exequies, provided the deceased was the subject of this pastor.[137] If the deceased was not the subject of the pastor, the local superior may conduct the funeral services in his own church.[138]

As an addendum to this discussion of the local superior's rights in connection with ecclesiastical burial, it is to be noted that he has certain rights with reference to the reconciliation of violated cemeteries. The rules of the canons concerning the reconciliation of churches apply also to the reconciliation of cemeteries.[139] A church (or cemetery) that was merely blessed can be reconciled by its rector, i.e., by the local superior who is the rector of the religious church.[140] In case of serious or urgent need the church (or cemetery) that is consecrated can be reconciled, if the ordinary cannot be reached, by the rector or the local superior. The local superior, however, must then inform the ordinary of his action.[141]

The Code also grants to the local superior rights in reference to the obligation of the wearing of the clerical garb and of the observance of the cloister. In urgent cases the local superior may judge that his subjects are excused from wearing the religious habit.[142] The cases would probably be quite rare when the local superior would make use of this power. Canon 596 does not refer to the temporary laying aside of the habit in accord

136 *PCI,* 20 iul, 1929 — *AAS,* XXI (1929), 573; Bouscaren, *The Canon Law Digest,* I, 572.

137 Can. 1230, § 4.

138 Abbo-Hannan, *The Sacred Canons,* II, 487.

139 Can. 1207.

140 Can. 1176, § 1; cf. Schaefer, *De Religiosis,* p. 823, n. 1380.

141 Can. 1176, § 3; cf. De Carlo, *Jus Religiosorum,* pp. 68, 18°; 364, III.

142 Can. 596.

with the approved custom of the country, as for example during the time of strenuous athletic recreation.[143] It refers rather to a prolonged practice of not wearing the religious habit, for example, in view of traveling through regions severely hostile to religion.

The local superior must provide that the episcopal enclosure demanded of non-exempt clerical Congregations by canons 604-606[144] is observed according to the letter and spirit of the law. The permission granted in canon 604 to superiors to admit women other than those mentioned in canons 598, § 2, and 600 may be exercised by the local superior for just and reasonable motives, e.g., in the visits from relatives, friends or benefactors.[145]

Since the local superior possesses dominative power over his subjects[146] he can validly, and for a just cause, lawfully annul a private[147] non-reserved[148] vow made by one of his subjects. The obligation of a vow which has been thus annulled never subsequently revives.[149] Similarly, the local superior has the same power over the promissory oaths of his subjects. If, however, the annulment should result in harm to others who refuse to condone an obligation, then only the Apostolic See is competent to grant a dispensation.[150]

Two grave obligations of the local superior are imposed by the Code when it deals with the processes of beatification and canonization.[151] The local superior is under grave obligation to see that all his subjects who are obliged to testify in such

---

143 Augustine notes in his *Commentary,* III, 307, that "on days when the mercury occasionally shows more than 100 degrees, the contrary custom (of not wearing the habit) may be adopted without misgiving."

144 Cf. De Carlo, *Jus Religiosorum,* p. 308, n. 369.

145 Augustine, *Commentary,* III, 319; Schaefer, *De Religiosis,* p. 706, n. 1188.

146 Can. 501, § 1.

147 Cf. can, 1308, § 1.

148 Cf. can, 1308, § 3.

149 Cf. can. 1312, § 1.

150 Can. 1320.

151 Cans. 2026; 2043, § 2; cf. De Carlo, *Jus Religiosorum,* p. 67, 11°.

processes do so. He must, however, beware of urging them either directly or indirectly to testify in one manner rather than in another.[152] Thus, the superior is strictly forbidden to influence his subjects to conceal the faults of a servant of God and speak only of his good characteristics, or *vice versa*.[153] If the servant of God belonged to his Institute, the local superior is under grave obligation to see to the publication in his own house of the edict requesting that all the writings of the servant of God be sent to the tribunal of the local ordinary. He must also make explicit mention of the requirements of canon 2025, § 2, namely, that his subjects shall transmit such writings either directly to the local ordinary or to the promoter of the faith, or hand them to their confessor, who shall forward them as soon as possible to the ordinary or to the promoter of the faith.[154]

As noted earlier, [155] the local superior is bound by the obligation of residence,[156] and thus, for obvious reasons, the obligation to conduct a canonical visitation of his own house is not imposed on him. In carrying out, however, his general obligations to see that his subjects observe the prescriptions of the common life and the Constitutions of the Institute, the superior will oftentimes find it useful to conduct an inspection of all the parts of his house. Such a tour of inspection could include a visit to the rooms or cells of his subjects to observe whether the laws of the common life with regard to furniture and clothing are being observed.[157] He should visit the kitchen, the laundry, the furnace room, in order to inspect the condition of the equipment and, in the event of any need, to arrange for its repair. The bursar ought to inform the superior about these matters, but the superior's firsthand knowledge of all the affairs of his house will

---

[152] Can. 2026.

[153] Stanislaus Woywod, *A Practical Commentary on the Code of Canon Law* (revised by Callistus Smith, revised and enlarged edition, 2 vols., New York: Joseph F. Wagner, Inc., 1948), II, 405.

[154] Can. 2043, § 2.

[155] Supra, pp. 75-77.

[156] Can. 508.

[157] Cf. can. 594.

enable him to make a more prudent judgment on the course of action to be followed in the settling of the various problems.

The role of the local superior in the canonical visitation conducted by the provincial superior must be one of co-operation and assistance. Severe penalties are established for the local superior who interferes with such a visitation.[158] The local superior must show a similar spirit of co-operation in connection with the visitation which the local ordinary is empowered to make. The Code grants the local ordinary the right to conduct a visitation every five years in every clerical Congregation of pontifical approval in regard to the church, the sacristy, the public oratory, and the confessionals.[159] The local superior must respect this right and must not interfere with the ordinary's exercise of his right.

The power to dismiss his subjects is granted to the local superior only in the case of grave scandal or of very serious imminent injury to the community. He can exercise this right only if there is danger in delay and time does not permit recourse to the major superior. If these circumstances are verified, the local superior, with the consent of his council, and of the local ordinary, may dismiss a delinquent subject. The whole matter, however, must be referred to the Holy See without delay, either by the local ordinary or by the major superior, if he be present.[160]

The local superior, working in conjunction with his provincial superior, should assiduously strive to reconcile a subject who may unfortunately have apostatized or fled from the religious life.[161] Motivated by the charity of Christ, he should consult with the proper authorities and be ready to take whatever measures are possible to receive the truly repentant.[162]

---

158 Can. 2413, §§ 1, 2.

159 Can. 512, § 2, 2°.

160 Can. 653.

161 Cf. can. 644.

162 Cf. can. 645, § 2.

The obligation to co-operate with the local ordinary and the pastors of the diocese in which the local superior's house is situated is stated in canon 608. The superior should exhort the subjects designated by him willingly to undertake assistance in the sacred ministry, especially in the diocese in which they live, as often as their services are needed by the ordinary or by the pastors. He must take care, however, that the religious discipline in his house does not suffer as a result of these works outside the community.

The local superior should furthermore be on guard lest the liturgical services in his church prove detrimental to the catechetical instruction or the explanation of the Gospel given in the parochial church. The local ordinary has the right to decide whether the services in the religious church are actually detrimental.[163]

Private exposition of the Blessed Sacrament in churches and oratories authorized to reserve the Blessed Sacrament is allowed for any just reason without the need of the ordinary's permission.[164] The local superior may give permission for this private exposition of the Blessed Sacrament in his church or oratory.[165]

The local superior has the right to bless those sacred furnishings which in accordance with liturgical laws must be blessed before they are used. The superior, or a priest of his Institute delegated by him, can bless such sacred furnishings for his own church or oratory.[166]

Article 2. The Authority of the Local Superior in Temporal Matters

The local superior's responsibilities regarding temporal matters may be classified under two headings: his obligations regarding the temporal goods possessed by his subjects; and his obligations regarding the temporal goods possessed by the community.

---

163 Can. 609.

164 Cf. can. 1274, § 1.

165 De Carlo, *Jus Religiosorum,* p. 68, 20°.

166 Can. 1304, 5°.

In dealing with the first of these responsibilities, one must of necessity recall certain principles which govern the simple vow of poverty. In non-exempt Congregations, unless the Constitutions declare otherwise, every professed religious retains the ownership of his property, as well as the capacity to acquire ownership of other property.[167] Before, however, making his profession of simple vows, a novice must cede the administration of his property to whomsoever he wishes. Unless the Constitutions provide otherwise, he may designate the use to which his property is to be put, and the purpose to which the income from it is to be allocated.[168] Absolute freedom is enjoyed by the novice in naming his administrator, and the local superior may not restrict the free exercise of this right. The novice is allowed to name the religious Institute as administrator if it is willing to accept the responsibility.[169] The local superior, in the name of his Institute, could agree to such an arrangement only after he had obtained the consent of his major superior. If no administrator was appointed at the time of his profession, inasmuch as the religious then did not possess any property, he must appoint one if he subsequently acquires property.[170] The local superior should make sure that his subjects fulfill this obligation. Once the subject has disposed of his property according to the prescriptions of canon 569, he cannot make changes or modifications in these arrangements unless the Constitutions allow him to do so.[171] The local superior has no authority to allow such changes, since the Code states that the Superior General alone is competent to grant permission in these matters.[172]

Not only must the novice appoint someone to administer his property, but he must also draw up a will in which he disposes of all the property which he owns or may come to own in the

---

[167] Can. 580, § 1.

[168] Can. 569, § 1.

[169] Creusen, *Religious*, p. 166, n. 217, 2; Abbo-Hannan, *The Sacred Canons*, I, 586.

[170] Can. 569, § 2.

[171] Can. 580, § 3.

[172] Can. 580, § 3.

future.[173] If the will had been made by a novice who was legally a minor, the local superior should take all necessary steps to insure that the formalities required by the civil law for the validity of wills are observed when the subject comes of age.[174] Permission to change the terms of a will is to be obtained from the Holy See. The local superior can permit a change in the will only in an emergency when there is no time to consult the Holy See or the major superior.[175] Modifications may be made in the will without the permission of the Holy See if the beneficiary has predeceased the testator, or if ratifying and explanatory codicils are added to the will to make its meaning clearer.[176] If the subject made no will before he made his profession, the superior should see to it that this omission is rectified. No permission of the Holy See is required in this case, since canon 583, 2°, merely forbids the making of a change in the will.[177] In offering assistance in the drawing up of the will, the local superior should avoid any and every undue influence which might persuade his subject to make the religious Institute the beneficiary. He should instruct his subject that he has complete freedom in his choice of beneficiary.[178]

The responsibilities of the local superior regarding gifts received by his subjects deserves consideration. Such a study requires an examination of canon 580, which states the basic principles to be applied in the solution of questions concerning gifts. In virtue of this canon, a religious who has professed simple vows retains the capacity to acquire additional personal property, unless the Constitutions forbid it. It is also stated in canon 580 that whatever the religious acquires by his own in-

---

173 Can. 569, § 3.

174 Schaefer, *De Religiosis,* p. 528, n. 928; Vermeersch-Creusen, *Epitome,* I, p. 531, n. 716.

175 Can. 563, § 2.

176 Fanfani, *De Iure Religiosorum,* p. 399, n. 256, 2°; Schaefer, *De Religiosis,* pp. 572-573, n. 984; Vermeersch-Creusen, *Epitome,* I, p. 550, n. 734.

177 Fanfani, *De Iure Religiosorum,* p. 399, n. 256, 2°.

178 Larraona, "Commentarium Codicis," *CpRM,* XXVIII (1949), 34, I, 3).

dustry, or by gift conferred in consideration of his status as a religious, belongs to his Institute. Thus gifts which are received may be intended for the religious personally *(intuitu personæ)* or for his community *(intuitu religionis).*[179] Whatever is given to the religious, not because he is a religious, but inasmuch as he is a private person, and apart from any consideration of his religious state, is intended for him as a personal gift. Thus, large gifts which come by way of inheritance or legacy, not because the recipient is a member of a Congregation, but rather because he is a personal friend or relative of the donor, are acquired by the religious as a person *(intuitu personæ).* Such gifts belong to him. Because, however, of the prescriptions of canon 569 he cannot use them for his own benefit, nor can he dispose of them freely. He is obliged to add them to his capital goods, which are to be cared for by the administrator he has appointed. Approved Constitutions which remove or restrict the capacity of religious to acquire new personal property are not contrary to canon 580. This canon expressly provides for such contrary provisions. If the Constitutions completely remove the capacity to acquire property, every gift received by the religious becomes the property of the Institute.

Gifts received by a religious inasmuch as he is a religious *(intuitu religionis)* are acquired by his religious community. If the motive of the donor was to foster the good works of the religious Institute or to show his special affection for the society, then the gift was made *intuitu religionis.* Such gifts, according to canon 580, §2, are to be turned over to the common goods of the community. The subject has no right to them.

There may be some difficulty in determining whether small gifts or money which are received on the occasion of birthdays or holidays are intended for the religious as a person or as a religious. It seems that presumptions should be invoked to determine the intention of the donor. If the gift is given with the

---

[179] Cf. Ellis, "Gifts to Religious, III, Personal *Versus* Community Property," *Review for Religious* (Topeka, Kansas, 1942-), VII (1948), 79.

words, "Get something for yourself," or "This is for you personally," it can be presumed that the donor wished his gift to be of some immediate value to his friend in religion. If the gift is considered as a personal gift *(intuitu personæ),* it must be added to the patrimony of the religious and can be of no benefit to him. The only way in which the gift can be of immediate value to the religious obtains when one may consider it as having been given *intuitu religionis.* It is then acquired by the community and is added to the common funds. The local superior who has charge of such goods may then grant permission to his subject to use the gift, provided that the virtue of poverty and the prescriptions of the common life are not violated. The superior, however, is not obliged to give the use of the gift to the subject who received it. It belongs to the common goods of the community, so that the subject has no claim to its use, unless the local superior gives permission.

Thus, in summary: no matter how a gift is given, whether as a personal gift, or for the community, the religious loses control of the use of it. It goes either to his patrimony or capital goods, of which he cannot dispose, or to the common goods of the community, which he cannot use except with his superior's permission.

The local superior should carefully explain to his subjects the provision of Canon Law concerning their capacity to acquire property. He should further explain the rules and regulations on this same matter as stated in the Constitutions of his Institute.

The superior as head of his community is guardian and custodian of the goods of the community. To him falls the obligation to see that these goods are distributed justly according to the needs of his subjects. He is to provide for their food, clothing, furniture and other necessities, adopting as his standard: "Let there be nothing superfluous in this matter and let nothing that is needed be denied."[180] The superior is furthermore obliged to enforce the observance of the common life. He is to insist

180 Ellis, "Gifts to Religious, II, Common Life and Peculium," *Review for Religious,* VII (1948), 39.

that the regulations on poverty and the common life proper to his own Institute are carried out regarding both the letter and the spirit of the law.[181]

The superior should consider the needs of his subject; he should not concern himself with the financial background of the relatives or friends of the subject. Thus, for example, the simple fact that the article requested by the subject can be obtained from a friend of the subject at no expense to the community should not enter into the superior's consideration of the subject's request. If the subject needs the article, and if the community can supply it, the superior should grant the request. If the need is not there, the request should be refused.

Upon this discussion of the local superior's obligation regarding the temporal goods of his subjects, it is necessary to examine his obligations regarding the temporal goods possessed by the community. The capacity of the religious house to acquire and possess temporal property is established in canon 531. This canon declares that not only the religious Institute itself, but also every province and every house, is capable of acquiring and possessing property with fixed or endowed revenue, unless this capacity is excluded or restricted by the Rules and Constitutions of the Institute. This provision is but a declaration of the general principle stated in canon 1495, § 2, namely that rights in regard to temporal matters are enjoyed by every moral entity which has been invested by ecclesiastical authority with juridical personality. The canonically erected house enjoys juridical personality, but it is unable, of itself, to administer its own goods. They are to be administered according to the Constitutions by the local superior and by those persons who have been lawfully appointed for that purpose.[182]

The administration of goods includes all those acts which contemplate the rightful preservation and improvement of the community's temporal goods according to their purpose and their

[181] Cf. can. 594.

[182] Can. 532, § 1.

nature.[183] In order to administer properly the temporal goods of his house, the local superior should be very familiar with his Constitutions. They are his first guide of action[184] along with the general laws of the Code governing the administration of property. Thus, by the common law, the administrator of the goods of a religious house is bound: (1) to conserve the goods of the house, keeping in mind the regulations of both canon and civil law; (2) to collect whatever rents or other returns are due for the use of the community's goods; (3) to keep a well-ordered account of the income and expenses of the house; (4) to safeguard documents, papers, and titles concerning the property of the house, and (5) to forward copies of these to the provincial archives, if the Constitutions so demand.[185]

Fully cognizant of the numerous duties which have been imposed on the local superior in his care for the spiritual welfare of his subjects, the legislator wisely provides for the appointment in each religious house of a procurator. He discharges his office under the direction of the local superior.[186] While a greater part of the actual administration of the goods will be done by the procurator, the superior cannot in conscience relinquish his obligation of vigilance.

In this regard, he will require of his procurator a full and complete account of all transactions entered into, and will give instructions with regard to the matters which he wishes attended to. If need be, he must correct or even punish the negligences of his procurator.

The Code allows the local superior to perform acts of ordinary administration.[187] Such acts include those financial transactions which occur frequently and are necessary for the

---

183 Creusen, *Religious,* p. 116, n. 156, 1.

184 Can. 532, § 1; cf. Vermeersch-Creusen, *Epitome,* I, p. 487, n. 655; Coronata, *Institutiones,* I, p. 692, n. 559.

185 Can. 1523.

186 Can. 516, § 2.

187 Can. 532, § 2.

daily sustenance and maintenance of the house itself.[188] These acts may be specified in the Constitutions or in the general or provincial chapters,[189] and usually include the buying of the things necessary for the current needs of the house, the collection of debts, the banking of sums of money, and the ordinary expenses for the upkeep of the property. The Constitutions should determine in what specific cases the local superior needs the counsel or consent of his councillors before undertaking acts of ordinary administration.

Extraordinary administration refers to those acts for which a special authorization must be received by the administrator from a higher authority in order that he may act validly.[190] They are generally acts which have as their object the disposition of capital or the undertaking of large debts, and which thus affect the financial stability of the house. Accordingly, investment and alienation of the goods of the house are acts of extraordinary administration.[191] Extraordinary administration embraces also the expenditure of money for the extraordinary conservation or improvement of the temporal goods of the house, such as the extraordinary repairs of a building.[192] All such acts of extraordinary administration lie beyond the competence of the local superior.[193] He cannot perform these acts unless he be authorized to do so.

As noted above, the investment of the goods of the community is an act of extraordinary administration, and therefore the local superior must have the approbation of the proper superiors before proceeding to invest money belonging to his house. The investment of money means the disposition of it in such a

---

188 Augustine, *Commentary*, III, 179; Coronata, *Institutiones*, I, p. 692, n. 559; Vermeersch-Creusen, *Epitome*, I, p. 487, n. 655; Abbo-Hannan, *The Sacred Canons*, I, p. 546, n. 532, 2.

189 Larraona, "Commentarium Codicis," *CpR*, XII (1931), 356, nota 481.

190 Larraona, "Commentarium Codicis," *CpR*, XII (1931), 357, IV.

191 Schaefer, *De Religiosis*, p. 380, n. 713.

192 O'Brien, *The Provincial Religious Superior*, pp. 167-168.

193 Clancy, *The Local Religious Superior*, p. 72.

manner as to assure that it will be preserved, at least in an equivalent form, and produce revenue.[194] Money deposited in a bank at a low rate of interest is not considered as invested, for the depositor is at liberty to withdraw the funds at any time.[195] A bank deposit serves more like a means for the protection of the money than as an investment of the money thus protected.[196]

If the money which the local superior wishes to invest has been donated or bequeathed to the house for expenditure in behalf of local divine worship or for local charities, he is required to obtain not only the consent of the higher superiors but also the consent of the local ordinary.[197] If the donor of the money to be invested has offered his gift, not to a particular religious house, but rather to the province or to the Institute as a whole, the consent of the ordinary is not required.[198] However, the ordinary's permission is to be obtained if the money to be invested has been given to a religious house, for example as a foundation for Masses, or as a burse for needy students.[199]

Special rules must be observed in connection with the reception and investment of a pious foundation for Masses. The local superior cannot accept foundations of this kind without the written permission of the local ordinary.[200] The money and the movable goods which are made a part of the endowment shall be immediately deposited in a safe place designated by the local ordinary.[201]

When money has been given by the faithful to a parish or a mission for parochial purposes, the superior, if he be the

---

194 Creusen, *Religious,* p. 116, n. 156, 3.

195 Coronata, *Institutiones,* I, p. 693, n. 593, 2°; Augustine, *Commentary,* III, 181; T. Lincoln Bouscaren-Adam Ellis, *Canon Law* (2. rev. ed., Milwaukee: The Bruce Publishing Co., 1951), p. 251.

196 Vermeersch-Creusen, *Epitome,* I, p. 486, n. 652.

197 Can. 533, § 1, 3°.

198 De Carlo, *Jus Religiosorum,* p. 163, n. 209, 3°, b); Beste, *Introductio in Codicem,* p. 336; Schaefer, *De Religiosis,* p. 365, n. 719.

199 Brys, *Juris Canonici Compendium,* I, 528, nota 3; Vermeersch-Creusen, *Epitome,* I, p. 488, n. 656, 2.

200 Can. 1546, § 1.

201 Can. 1547.

pastor, must also obtain the permission of the local ordinary before he can invest such funds.[202] The term "mission" in this context indicates a quasi-parish in the sense of canon 216, § 3, as well as any parish subdivision not formally established as a parish.[203] Thus, if the local superior wishes to *invest* money received from pew-rent, church collections and the like, he must have the consent of the local ordinary, since the investment of these funds is an act of extraordinary administration and requires the ordinary's permission.[204] Not only must the local superior obtain the permission of the local ordinary to invest the funds given to his house for local divine worship or for local charities, or to the parish or mission for parochial purposes, but he must also respect the rights granted to the local ordinary to inquire into the administration of such funds.[205]

Alienation is also an act of extraordinary administration,[206] and thus the local superior cannot without the permission of the higher superiors validly alienate any of the goods belonging to the house. Alienation may be defined as any act by which there is a transfer of ownership of ecclesiastical property to another proprietor. It includes any contract made by an ecclesiastical moral person when through such a contract the ecclesiastical property of that person becomes less secure.[207] Thus the laws governing alienation are applied alike to onerous contracts and to the contracting of debts and financial obligations.

In the alienation of any ecclesiastical property, the common law demands that certain formalities are to be observed. There is required: 1) a written appraisal from reliable experts regarding the property to be alienated; 2) a just cause for the aliena-

---

[202] Can. 533, § 1, 4°.

[203] Berutti, *Institutiones,* III, p. 118, n. 58, 3; De Carlo, *Jus Religiosorum,* p. 160, n. 206, I, 1; Abbo-Hannan, *The Sacred Canons,* I, 548.

[204] Augustine, *Commentary,* III, 182.

[205] Can. 532, § 3, 2°.

[206] Schaefer, *De Religiosis,* p. 380, n. 713.

[207] Schaefer, *De Religiosis,* p. 388, n. 725; Creusen, *Religious,* p. 116, n. 156, 1; William Doheny, *Practical Problems in Church Finance* (Milwaukee: The Bruce Publishing Company, 1941), p. 21.

tion; and 3) the permission of the proper superior.[208] Unless circumstances make a different procedure the preferable one to follow, the property must be sold to the highest bidder, at or beyond the price of the appraisal, and the money received through the act of alienation must be prudently invested.[209]

The local superior is always required to have the permission of the proper superior for the validity of his acts when these involve the alienation of the goods of his house. The Holy See is the authority from whom permission must be obtained if the amount of the alienation exceeds 10,000 gold francs (5,000 American or Canadian dollars).[210] If the amount is less than that sum, the permission of the superior designated by the Constitutions is required.

In the petition for permission to contract debts or obligations, the local superior is obliged to state the total amount of other debts currently burdening the religious house, for otherwise the obtained permission remains void.[211]

A warning is issued to religious superiors in canon 536. If the local superior contracts debts and obligations without the required authorization of the Constitutions or the needed permission of his superiors, he himself is responsible, and not the

---

208 Can. 1530, § 1.

209 Can. 1531.

210 Cf. can. 534, which states that, if the value of the religious property to be alienated exceeds 30,000 francs, the permission of the Holy See is required. On July 31, 1951, the 30,000 franc limit indicated in canon 534 was reduced to 10,000 gold francs (*AAS* XLIII [1951], 602). On January 29, 1953, the Sacred Congregation for Religious published the equivalents of 10,000 gold francs for the principal countries of the world. The equivalent for the United States and Canada is given as 5,000 dollars. As matters now stand, therefore, the permission of the Holy See must be obtained for the alienating of property or the incurring of a debt when the amount exceeds 5,000 dollars in ordinary American or Canadian currency (Cf. *Review for Religious,* XII [1953], 134).

211 Can. 543, § 2; cf. Letter of the Apostolic Delegate to the United States, Nov. 13, 1936 — Bouscaren, *The Canon Law Digest,* II, 164-165, IV.

religious house.[212] In addition, severe penalties are to be imposed on the local superior who violates the provisions of canons 534 and 1532 regarding alienation.[213] The greatest penalty is that of excommunication, though not reserved for its absolution. A religious superior who has illegally alienated property valued at more than one thousand francs shall be deprived of his office and eligibility to acquire any other office. In addition he is to be punished with appropriate penalties to be imposed by his superiors.

Canon 537 limits the bestowal of gifts to almsgiving and other just causes, with the permission of the local superior and in keeping with the Constitutions. The local superior may give permission to his subjects to offer gifts if the two conditions stated in canon 537 are verified. Helping the poor by almsgiving is an act of virtue and is always a good reason.[214] A just reason for making moderate donations may also originate from the rightful desire to show gratitude to benefactors or to those who have rendered service.[215] The Constitutions and legitimate customs may serve as guides for the local superior in these matters. The superior himself in giving gifts should remember that he is merely the administrator and not the owner of the goods of the community. For this reason his own donations should be moderated in accordance with the Constitutions and customary usage.

By way of conclusion to this discussion of the rights and duties of the local superior in temporal matters, some reference to the decree *"Pluribus ex documentis"* is in order.[216] The decree notes that clerics have always been forbidden by the Church, under threat of grave penalties and censures, to engage in worldly occupations, especially in business and trade. It observes that the Code of Canon Law, by canon 142, forbids clerics to conduct

---

212 Can. 536, § 3.

213 Can. 2347.

214 Cf. Papi, *The Government of Religious Communities*, p. 185.

215 Cf. Augustine, *Commentary*, III, 196, b).

216 S. C. C., 22 mart. 1950 — *AAS*, XLII (1950), 330-331.

business or trade, either personally or through agents, either for their own benefit or for that of other persons. By way of penal sanction, the decree states that any cleric or religious who engages in trade or business of any kind, whether it be for his own benefit or that of others, in violation of canon 142, incurs *ipso facto* an excommunication reserved *speciali modo* to the Apostolic See. In extreme cases degradation may even be decreed. Superiors, moreover, who have not prevented the commission of such crimes, in so far as their office and authority permitted, are to be removed from office and declared incapable of holding in the future any governing or administrative positions. The local superior clearly has the obligation to make himself familiar with the provisions and practical application of canon 142.[217]

[217] Cf. Joseph Brunini, *The Clerical Obligations of Canons 139 and 142,* The Catholic University of America Canon Law Studies, n. 103 (Washington, D.C.: The Catholic University of America, 1937); A. Gutierrez, "Studia Canonica," *CpRM* XXXI (1950), 183-211; XXXII (1951), 151-159; Thomas Smiddy, "Negotiatio," *The Jurist,* XI (1951), 486-519; W. Conway, "Important New Decree on *Negotiatio,*" *Irish Ecclesiastical Record* (Dublin, 1864-), 5. series, LXXIV (1950), 366-371; "*Negotiatio,* The New Decree," *ibidem,* pp. 444-445, 537; "*Negotiatio*: Sale of Shares," "*Negotiatio*: Sale of Pious Objects, Candles, Books," *Irish Ecclesiastical Record,* 5. series, LXXV (1951), 69-71; Hannan, "Cases and Studies," *The Jurist,* XI (1951), 102-104; Joseph Donovan, "Questions Answered," *The Homiletic and Pastoral Review* (New York, 1900- [1900-1917: *Homiletic Monthly and Catechist;* 1917-1918: *Homiletic Monthly;* 1918-1920: *Homiletic Monthly and Pastoral Review*]), LI (1951), 85-86; 373-374, (1).

CONCLUSIONS

1. Before the promulgation of the Code of Canon Law there was no common law that governed Congregations in which the members took simple vows (pp. 16-27).

2. Each canonically erected religious house in a non-exempt Congregation is constituted an imperfect society. The head of that society must possess authority to rule over the members (pp. 29, 32).

3. The dominative power possessed by the local superior has its basis in the fact that the superior is the head of a society lawfully established by the Church (pp. 41-42).

4. Dominative power, though it is distinct from ecclesiastical jurisdiction, enshrines a public power of ruling and differs profoundly from the private power of ruling exercised by the heads of amicable societies (pp. 44-47).

5. All the faculties attributed by the Code to superiors in non-exempt Congregations are an expression of the dominative power which, according to canon 501, § 1, is possessed by religious superiors (pp. 48-59).

6. The disqualifying provisions of canon 504 apply to the appointment of major superiors only; they cannot equally be urged against the appointment of a local superior (pp. 60-61).

7. A religious who is simultaneously appointed to two compatible offices when to each of them is attached the obligation of making the profession of faith need make only one

profession of faith, provided that a testimonial in proof of his making the profession is shown to the person who would otherwise have the right to demand another making of the same profession (pp. 73-75).

8. The expression "members of the household" *(familiares)* as used in canon 509, § 2, 2°, includes all the persons listed in canon 514, § 1. Therefore, the local superior is bound to provide for an instruction in Christian doctrine to be given to all those who dwell day and night in the religious house by reason of domestic service, education, hospitality or for the purpose of recovering their health (pp. 85-86).

9. The obligation to provide a pious exhortation at least twice a month to all the members of the community rests on the local superior of a non-exempt clerical Congregation (p. 86).

BIBLIOGRAPHY

SOURCES

Acta Apostolicae Sedis, Commentarium Officiale, Romae, 1909-1929; Civitate Vaticana, 1929-

Acta et Decreta Sacrorum Conciliorum Recentiorum, Collectio Lacensis, 7 vols., Friburgi Brisgoviae, 1870-1892.

Acta Sanctae Sedis, 41 vols., Romae, 1865-1908.

Bouscaren, T. Lincoln, *The Canon Law Digest,* 2 vols. and Supplement through 1948, Milwaukee: The Bruce Publishing Co., 1934, 1943, 1949.

Bullarum Diplomatum et Privilegiorum Romanorum Pontificum Taurinensis Editio, 24 vols. et Appendix, Augustae Taurinorum, 1857-1872.

Bullarii Romani Continuatio Summorum Pontificum, 19 vols. in 20, Prati, 1835-1857.

Codex Iuris Canonici Pii X Pontificis Maximi iussu digestus, Benedicti Papae XV auctoritate promulgatus, Praefatione, Fontium Annotatione et Indice Analytico-Alphabetico ab Emo Petro Card. Gasparri auctus, Romae: Typis Polyglottis Vaticanis, 1917.

Codicis Iuris Canonici Fontes, cura Emi Petri Card. Gasparri editi, 9 vols., Romae (postea Civitate Vaticana): Typis Polyglottis Vaticanis, 1923-1939. (Vols. VII-IX, ed. cura et studio Emi Iustiniani Card. Serédi).

Collectanea in Usum Secretariae Sacrae Congregationis Episcoporum et Regularium, cura A. Bizzarri Archiepiscopi Philippensis Secretarii edita, 2. ed., Romae: Ex Typis Polyglotta, S. C. de Propaganda Fide, 1885.

Constitutions and Rules of the Congregation of the Missionary Oblates of the Most Holy and Immaculate Virgin Mary, The, Rome, 1945.

Corpus Iuris Canonici, ed. Lipsiensis secunda, post Aemilii Richteri curas... instruxit Aemilius Friedberg, 2 vols., Lipsiae, 1879-1881.

Decretales D. Gregorii Papae IX, suae integritati una cum glossis restitutae, cum privilegio Gregorii XIII, Pont. Max., et aliorum Principium, Romae, 1582.

Decretum Gratiani emendatum et notationibus illustratum cum glossis, Gregorii XIII, Pont. Max., iussu editum, 2 vols., Romae, 1582.

Liber Sextus Decretalium D. Bonifacii Papae VIII, suae integritati cum Clementinis et Extravagantibus, earumque Glossis restitutis, Romae, 1582.

Mansi, Joannes, *Sacrorum Conciliorum Nova et Amplissima Collectio,* 53 vols. in 60, Parisiis, 1901-1927.

Normae Secundum Quas S. Cong. Episcoporum et Regularium procedere solet in approbandis Novis Institutis Votorum Simplicium, Romae: Typis S. C. De Propaganda Fide, 1901.

Reference Works

Acta Congressus Iuridici Internationalis, 5 vols., Romae: Apud Custodiam Librariam Pont. Instituti Utriusque Iuris, 1935-1937.

Abbo, John — Hannan, Jerome, *The Sacred Canons,* 2 vols., St. Louis: B. Herder Book Co., 1952.

Aristotle, *Omnia Opera,* Graece et Latine, 2 vols., Parisiis: Editoribus Firmin-Didot et Sociis, 1883.

Augustine, Charles, *A Commentary on the New Code of Canon Law,* 8 vols., Vol. II, 3. ed., 1919; Vol. III, 4. ed., 1929; St. Louis: B. Herder Book Co.

Balmes, Hilaire, *Les Religieux à voeux simples d'après le Code,* Paray-le-Monial: Au Secrétariat des Oeuvres du Sacré-Coeur, 1921.

Battandier, Albert, *Guide Canonique pour les Constitutions des Instituts à Voeux Simples,* 6. ed., Paris, 1923.

Benedictus XIV, Pont. Max., *De Synodo Dioecesana,* 3 vols., Romae: Ex Typographia Jo. Baptistae Cannetti, 1783.

Berutti, Christophorus, *Institutiones Iuris Canonici,* 6 vols. in 7, Vol. III, *De Religiosis,* Taurini-Romae: Marietti, 1936.

Beste, Udalricus, *Introductio in Codicem,* 3. ed., Collegeville, Minn.: St. John's Abbey Press, 1946.

Biederlack, J. — Führich, M., *De Religiosis,* Oeniponte: Rauch, 1919.

Blat, Albertus, *Commentarium Textus Codicis Iuris Canonici,* 5 vols. in 6, Lib. II, *Ius de Religiosis,* 3. ed., Romae: "apud Angelicum," 1938.

Bouix, Dominicus, *Tractatus de Iure Regularium,* 3. ed., 2 vols., Parisiis, 1882-1883.

Bouscaren, T. Lincoln — Ellis, Adam, *Canon Law,* 2 rev. ed., Milwaukee: The Bruce Publishing Co., 1951.

Bowe, Thomas, *Religious Superioresses,* The Catholic University of America Canon Law Studies, n. 228, Washington, D.C.: The Catholic University of America Press, 1946.

Brockhaus, Thomas Aquinas, *Religious Who Are Known as Conversi,* The Catholic University of America Canon Law Studies, n. 225, Washington, D.C.: The Catholic University of America Press, 1946.

Brunini, Joseph, *The Clerical Obligations of Canons 139 and 142,* The Catholic University of America Canon Law Studies, n. 103, Washington, D.C.: The Catholic University of America, 1937.

Brys, J., *Juris Canonici Compendium,* 10. ed., 2. ed. post Codicem, 2 vols., Brugis: Desclée de Brouwer et Sii, 1947-1949.

Canavan, Walter, *The Profession of Faith,* The Catholic University of America Canon Law Studies, n. 151, Washington, D.C.: The Catholic University of America Press, 1942.

Cance, Adrien, *Le Code de Droit Canonique,* 7. ed., 3 vols., Paris: J. Gabalda, 1946.

Cappello, Felix, *Summa Iuris Publici Ecclesiastici,* 2. ed., Romae: apud aedes Universitatis Gregorianae, 1928.

Chelodi, Ioannes, *Ius Canonicum de Personis,* 3. ed., curavit Pius Ciprotti, Vicenza: Società anonima tipografica; Trento: A. Ardesi, 1942.

Claeys Bouuaert, F. — Simenon, G., *Manuale Juris Canonici,* 3 vols., Vol. I, 5. ed., Gandae et Leodii: Prostat apud auctores in Seminariis Canavensi et Leodiensi, 1939.

Clancy, Patrick, *The Local Religious Superior,* The Catholic University of America Canon Law Studies, n. 171, Washington, D.C.: The Catholic University of America Press, 1943.

Cocchi, Guidus, *Commentarium in Codicem Iuris Canonici ad Usum Scholarum,* 8 vols., Vol. IV (Liber II, *De Personis,* Pars II, *De Religiosis*), 4. ed., Taurinorum Augustae: Ex Officina Libraria Marietti, 1946.

Coronata, Matthaeus Conte a, *Institutiones Iuris Canonici ad Usum Utriusque Cleri et Scholarum,* 5 vols., Vol. I and Vol. II, 2. ed., Taurini: Marietti, 1939.

Craisson, D., *Manuale Totius Juris Canonici,* 5. ed., 3 vols., Pictavii, 1877.

Creusen, Josephus, *De Iuridica Status Religiosi Evolutione,* 2. ed., Romae: Apud Aedes Pontificae Universitatis Gregorianae, 1948.

———, *Religieux et Religieuses d'après le Droit Ecclésiastique,* 6. ed., Paris: Desclée de Brouwer, 1950.

———, *Religious Men and Women in the Code,* 3. English ed. revised and edited to conform with 5. French ed. by Adam Ellis; first translation by Edward Garesché, Milwaukee: The Bruce Publishing Company, 1940.

De Carlo, Camillus, *Jus Religiosorum,* Parisiis-Tornaci-Romae: Desclée et Socii, 1950.

Doheny, William, *Practical Problems in Church Finance,* Milwaukee: The Bruce Publishing Company, 1941.

Donnellan, Thomas, *The Obligation of the Missa pro Populo,* The Catholic University of America Canon Law Studies, n. 155, Washington, D.C.: The Catholic University of America Press, 1942.

Fanfani, Ludovicus, *De Iure Religiosorum,* 3. ed., Rovigo: Istituto Padano di Arti Grafiche, 1949.

Gill, Nicholas, *The Spiritual Prefect in Clerical Religious Houses of Study,* The Catholic University of America Canon Law Studies, n. 216, Washington, D.C.: The Catholic University of America Press, 1945.

Goyeneche, Servus, *Iuris Canonici Summa Principia de Religiosis,* Roma: Tip. Pol. "Cuore di Maria," 1938.

Guido de Bayso, *In Decretorum Volumen Commentaria (Rosarium),* Venetiis, 1577.

Hale, Joseph, *The Pastor of Burial,* The Catholic University of America Canon Law Studies, n. 234, Washington, D.C.: The Catholic University of America Press, 1949.

Kindt, Gerardus, *De Potestate Dominativa in Religione,* Universitas Catholica Louvaniensis Dissertationes, Series II, Tomus 34, Brugis-Parisiis-Romae: Desclée de Brouwer, 1945.

Lewis, Gordian, *Chapters in Religious Institutes,* The Catholic University of Amercia Canon Law Studies, n. 181, Washington, D.C.: The Catholic University of America Press, 1943.

Maroto, Philippus, *Institutiones Iuris Canonici ad Normam Novi Codicis,* 2 vols., Romae: apud Commentarium pro Religiosis; Matriti: Editorial del Corazón de Maria, 1919.

Michiels, Gommarus, *Normae Generales Iuris Canonici, Commentarius Libri I Codicis Iuris Canonici,* 2. ed., 2 vols., Tornaci: Desclée et Socii, 1949.

Molitor, Raphael, *Religiosi Iuris Capita Selecta,* Ratisbonae, Neo-Eboraci et Cincinnati: Pustet, 1909.

Nervegna, I., *De Institutis Votorum Simplicium Religiosorum et Monialium,* Romae, 1904.

Nervegna, I., *De Iure Practico Regularium,* Romae, 1900.

O'Brien, Romaeus William, *The Provincial Religious Superior,* The Catholic University of America Canon Law Studies, n. 258, Washington, D.C.: The Catholic University of America Press, 1947.

Orth, Raymond, Clement, *The Approbation of Religious Institutes,* The Catholic University of America Canon Law Studies, n. 71, Washington, D.C.: The Catholic University of America, 1931.

Ottaviani, Alaphridus, *Institutiones Iuris Publici Ecclesiastici,* 3. ed., 2 vols., Civitate Vaticana: Typis Polyglottis Vaticanis, 1947.

Panormitanus, Abbas (Nicholaus de Tudeschis), *Commentaria in Quinque Libros Decretalium,* 5 vols. in 7, Venetiis, 1588.

Papi, Hector, *The Government of Religious Communities,* New York: P. J. Kenedy & Sons, 1919.

Pejska, Josephus, *Ius Canonicum Religiosorum,* 3. ed., Friburgi Brisgoviae: Herder & Co., 1927.

Piat, F. (Jean Joseph, Loiseaux), *Praelectiones Iuris Regularis,* 2. ed., Tornaci, 1896-1898.

Pirhing, Ernricus, *Ius Canonicum,* 5 vols. in 4, Dilingae, 1676.

Prümmer, Dominicus, *Manuale Iuris Canonici,* 5. ed., Friburgi-Brisgoviae: Herder, 1927.

Raus, J. B., *De Sacrae Obedientiae Virtute et Voto,* Lugduni: Vitte, 1923.

Rodrigo, Lucius, *Praelectiones Theologico-Morales Comillenses,* Vol. II, *De Legibus,* Santander: "Sal Terrae", 1944.

Rothoff, H., *Le Droit des Sociétés sans Voeux,* Bruges: Desclée de Brouwer, 1949.

Sanguineti, Sebastianus, *Iuris Ecclesiastici Privati Institutiones,* 3. ed., Romae, 1896.

Sebastianelli, G., *Praelectiones Iuris Canonici,* 3 vols., Vol. II, *De Personis,* 2. ed., Romae, 1905.

Schaefer, Timotheus, *De Religiosis,* 4. ed., Roma: Editrice "Apostolato Cattolico," 1947.

Schorr, George, *The Law of the Celebret,* The Catholic University of America Canon Law Studies, n. 332, Washington, D.C.: The Catholic University of America Press, 1952.

Schroeder, Henry J., *Disciplinary Decrees of the General Councils,* St. Louis: B. Herder Book Co., 1937.

Sipos, Stephanus, *Enchiridion Iuris Canonici,* Pécs, 1926.

Smith, Mariner, *The Penal Law for Religious,* The Catholic University of America Canon Law Studies, n. 98, Washington, D.C.: The Catholic University of America, 1935.

Stanton, W. A., *De Societatibus sive Virorum sive Mulierum in Communi Viventium sine Votis,* 2. ed., Halifaxiae: Apud Custodiam Librariam Maioris Seminarii a Sanctissimo Corde B.V.M., 1936.

Suarez, Franciscus, *Opera Omnia,* 28 vols., Parisiis, 1856-1878.

Thomas, St., *Doctoris Angelici Opera Omnia,* secundum impressionem Petri Fiaccadori Parmae 1852-1873 (photolithographice reimpressa), 25 vols., Vols. I-IV, *Summa Theologica,* New York: Musurga Publishers, 1948.

Toso, A., *Ad Codicem Iuris Canonici Commentaria Minora,* 5 vols., Romae, 1920-1927.

Turner, Sidney Joseph, *The Vow of Poverty,* The Catholic University of America Studies in Canon Law, n. 54, Washington, D.C.: The Catholic University of America, 1929.

Tyck, Charles, *Notices Historiques sur les Congrégations et Communautés Religieuses du XIXme Siècle,* Louvain, 1892.

Van Hove, Alphonsus, *Commentarium Lovaniense in Codicem Iuris Canonici,* 1 vol. in 5 tomis, Tom. II, *De legibus ecclesiasticis,* Mechliniae-Romae: H. Dessain, 1930.

Vermeersch, Arthurus — Creusen, Josephus, *Epitome Iuris Canonici,* 3 vols., Vol. I, 7. ed., Mechliniae-Romae: H. Dessain, 1949, Vol. III, 6. ed., Mechliniae-Romae: H. Dessain, 1946.

Woywod, Stanislaus, *A Practical Commentary on the Code of Canon Law,* revised by Callistus Smith, revised and enlarged edition, 2 vols., New York: Joseph F. Wagner, Inc., 1948.

Articles

Bastnagel, Clement, "Cases and Studies," *The Jurist,* X (1950), 52-55.

Blat, Albertus, "De Potestate Superiorum in Religionibus Secundum Codicem I. C.," *CpRM,* XVI (1935), 321-353.

Conway, W., "Important New Decree on *Negotiatio," Irish Ecclesiastical Record,* 5. series, LXXIV (1950), 366-371.

———, "*Negotiatio*: The New Decree," *Irish Ecclesiastical Record,* 5. series, LXXIV (1950), 444-445, 537.

———, "*Negotiatio*: Sale of Shares," "*Negotiatio*: Sale of Pious Objects, Candles, Books," *Irish Ecclesiastical Record,* 5. series, LXXV (1951), 69-71.

Delchard, P., "Elements of Canon Law," *Religious Sisters,* being the English version of *Directoire des Supérieures* and *Les Adaptations de la Vie Religieuse,* Westminster, Maryland: The Newman Press, 1951.

Donovan, Joseph, "Questions Answered," *Homiletic and Pastoral Review,* LI (1951), 85-86, 373-374.

Ellis, Adam, "Gifts to Religious, II. Common Life and Peculium," *Review for Religious,* VII (1948), 33-45.

———, "Gifts to Religious, III. Personal *Versus* Community Property," *Review for Religious,* VII (1948), 79-86.

Fuertes, J. B., "De Potestate Dominativa in Religionibus Non Exemptis," *CpRM,* XXXII (1953), 198-209, 274-279, 341-346.

Goyeneche, Servus, "Consultationes," *CpR,* III (1922), 217-219; XI (1930), 350-351; *CpRM,* XXII (1941), 24-25.

Gutierrez, A., "Studia Canonica," *CpRM,* XXXI (1950), 183-221, XXXII (1951), 151-159.

Hannan, Jerome, "Cases and Studies," *The Jurist,* XI (1951), 102-104.

Heston, Edward, "Some Aspect of Government in Religious Communities," *The Jurist,* X (1950), 35-51.

Jombart, E., "Subordination dans l'Exercise de l'Autorité," *Revue des Communautés Religieuses,* XI (1935), 69-75.

Larraona, Arcadius, "Commentarium Codicis," *CpR,* I (1920), 16-21, 45-50, 133-140, 171-177, 209-217, 345-349; VII (1926), 30-36, 376-391, 444-448; VIII (1927), 37-39; IX (1928), 204-211.

———, "De Potestate Dominativa Publica in Iure Canonico," *Acta Congressus Iuridici Internationalis,* Romae, IV, 145-180.

Smiddy, Thomas, "Negotiatio," *The Jurist,* XI (1951), 486-519.

Steiger, A. P., "De Propagatione et Diffusione Vitae Religiosae," *Periodica,* XIII (1924), (29)-(60), (73)-(100), (153)-(180).

Vermeersch, Arthurus, "Annotationes," *Periodica,* V (1911), 230-232.

———, "De Consiliariis Superiorum," *Periodica,* XV (1927), (61)-(63).

Periodicals

Commentarium pro Religiosis, Romae, 1920-1934; ab anno 1935: *Commentarium pro Religiosis et Missionariis.*

Homiletic and Pastoral Review, The, New York, 1900-(1900-1917: *Homiletic Monthly and Catechist;* 1917-1918: *Homiletic Monthly;* 1918-1920: *Homiletic Monthly and Pastoral Review*).

Irish Ecclesiastical Record, The, Dublin, 1864-

Jurist, The, Washington, D.C., 1941-

Periodica de Religiosis et Missionariis, Brugis, 1905-1919; ab anno 1920: *Periodica de Re Canonica et Morali, utilia praesertim Religiosis et Missionariis,* Brugis, 1920-1927; ab anno 1927: *Periodica de Re Morali, Canonica, Liturgica,* Brugis, 1927-1936, et Romae, 1937-

Review for Religious, Topeka, Kansas, 1942-

Revue des Communautés Religieuses, Enghien, Belgique, 1925-

ALPHABETICAL INDEX

BIOGRAPHICAL NOTE

Robert Eamon McGrath was born on January 20, 1922, in Saskatoon, Saskatchewan, Canada. He received his primary education at St. Joseph's Parochial School in Saskatoon, and his secondary education at St. Patrick's College, Ottawa, Ontario. In August, 1941, he entered the Novitiate of the Oblates of Mary Immaculate in Ottawa. His philosophical and theological courses he received at Holy Rosary Scholasticate in the same city. He was ordained to the Holy Priesthood on June 13, 1948, at the end of his third year of theology. After the completion of his theological course in 1949, he was assigned to teach at Holy Rosary Scholasticate. In September, 1951, he was sent by his Superiors to the Catholic University of America to pursue a course of graduate studies in the School of Canon Law. In June, 1952, he received the degree of Bachelor of Canon Law, and in June, 1953, he received the degree of Licentiate in Canon Law.

CANON LAW STUDIES *

349. BÖTTOMS, REV. ARCHIBALD M., J.C.L., The discretionary authority of the ecclesiastical judge in matrimonial trials of the first instance.
350. KEKUMANÖ, REV. CHARLES A., A.B., J.C.L., The secret archives of the diocesan curia.
351. MCGRATH, REV. ROBERT EAMON, O.M.I., J.C.L., The local superior in non-exempt clerical congregations.
352. MCMANUS, REV. FREDERICK RICHARD, A.B., J.C.L., The Congregation of Sacred Rites.
353. RODIMER, REV. FRANK J., A.B., S.T.L., J.C.L., The canonical effects of infamy of fact.
354. RÖUILLARD, REV. JACQUES, A.B., Ph.B., J.C.L., Une étude comparée du droit canonique et du droit civil paroissial de là Province de Québec dans l'administration des biens paroissiaux.
355. RYAN, REV. THOMAS C., J.C.L., The juridical effects of the *sanatio in radice*.
356. SULLIVAN, REV. BERNARD OWENS, J.C.L., Legislation and requirements for permissible cohabitation in invalid marriages.
357. TATARCZUK, REV. VINCENT ANTHÖNY, A.B., S.T.L., J.C.L., Infamy of law.

---

* For a complete list of the available numbers of this series apply to the Catholic University of America Press, 620 Michigan Ave., N. E., Washington 17, D.C., for a general catalogue.

www.ingramcontent.com/pod-product-compliance
Lightning Source LLC
LaVergne TN
LVHW050208080826
844660LV00012B/377

* 9 7 8 0 8 1 3 2 2 5 1 9 7 *